Spoolcraft

Spoolcraft

ARDEN J. NEWSOME

Illustrations by
Kathleen McGee and
Arden J. Newsome

Lothrop, Lee & Shepard Co.

NEW YORK

Contents

Spool Toys

Knitting and Printing With Spools

General Instructions

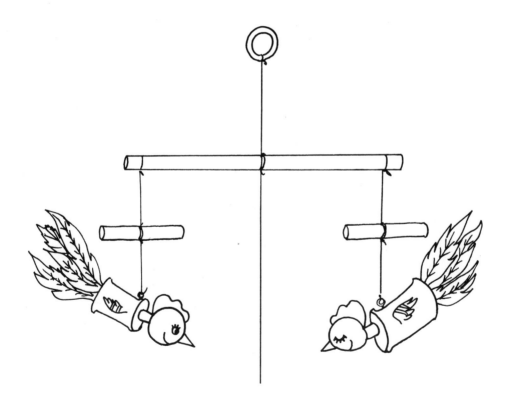

Getting Ready

Going on a treasure hunt to find materials is almost as much fun as making things. Here is a list of what to look for before you begin your spool projects:

1. A large cardboard box to hold your spools and other materials.
2. Empty wooden spools of all sizes and shapes. (Ask your mother and her friends, if they sew, to save the empties for you. Also sewing centers and stores that sell sewing machines will give you empty spools for the asking.)
3. Large beads of all sorts and sizes. Try craft shops for these as well as toy shops which have baby's bead-stringing sets. Cork balls may be used instead of beads.
4. Ribbons, felt and fabric scraps, odds and ends of trimmings such as braids, cotton tubing, sequins, and glitter.
5. Cardboard, string, gift wrapping paper and construction paper.
6. Blocks, squares, and rectangles of wood. Look in your father's workshop, if he has one, or investigate a local lumber yard or carpenter's scrap pile.
7. Dowel sticks—from many sources: lollipops, candy apples, balloons, ice cream sticks. Try hobby shops or lumber yard.
8. Medium and fine grain sandpaper and emery boards.
9. Plastic wood. (Natural color in a tube.)
10. A good white, liquid clear-drying glue such as Sobo glue.
11. Various kinds of paint.
12. Turpentine.
13. Tools: scissors, compass, a small saw, tack hammer, and a round file.

Get Acquainted with Your Materials First

It is a good idea to get acquainted with the various materials and tools you will be using before making any spool project.

Spools: Discover the many different sizes and shapes of spools and learn how to substitute one size for another. For instance: short spools, the size used for silk thread, are half the size of the common small thread spool. Therefore, a small spool sawed in half can often be substituted for two short spools. Possibly the only spools you cannot find a satisfactory substitute for are the very tiny ones found in mending kits.

Glue: Sobo is excellent for wood, paper, fabric, and practically all your craft projects. It forms a strong bond and although it is quick drying, you will find it does not dry so fast that you cannot make corrections.

An excellent way to apply glue is to use a small, inexpensive paintbrush. This method is easy and neat and almost ensures a thin smooth layer. Keep the brush in a small jar filled with a little water to keep it soft and pliable. Wash brush with soap and warm water when finished with it.

Always let glue dry completely before applying paint.

Paint: Wooden spools can be painted with almost any type of paint. You can use enamels left over from other projects, spray paints, tempera or poster paints. But the spools must be first sealed with a primer such as gesso or clear shellac. Because unfinished wood soaks up paint like a sponge, a primer must be applied to fill the pores of the wood and to prepare a suitable surface for paint. Gesso is an acrylic, waterproof, white primer that can be purchased wherever artist's supplies are sold. You can use almost any paint over gesso, including tempera and poster paint.

Tempera paints in jars are easy to use. However, they should be protected with a clear fixative such as colorless nail polish or clear plastic spray. A new type of poster paint, called acrylic poster color, dries waterproof and is an excellent paint for just about all spoolcraft projects. It comes with its own gloss medium which is a white liquid that dries clear and shiny. It can be mixed with the paint to give it a glossy shine and used as a final protective finish.

Paints of the same kind can be mixed to make many different colors. If you are using tempera paints, regular or acrylic, all you need is one jar of each of the following colors: red, yellow, blue, black, and white. From these colors you can make many more: red and yellow make orange, white with just a drop of red and yellow produces a flesh tone, red and blue make violet, and blue and yellow make green. Experiment with various colors to see what shades you can make. As you experiment you will learn just how much of each color should be used to produce another color, but, to begin with, mix only small amounts of each. Put a little in an old clean jar lid or in a plastic ice cube tray, then mix in another color. Adding white will lighten a color, and a drop of black will make the color darker. Always wash your brush when going from one color to another.

Paintbrushes: Your paintbrushes will last a long time if you take proper care of them. You do not have to purchase expensive artist brushes but cheap brushes do not perform well. Most stores that sell artist's supplies carry an inexpensive package of three brushes in three different sizes. The brushes have nicely rounded bristles and the three sizes will be the answer to most of your painting needs. Don't try to paint large areas with a tiny brush or tiny details and facial features with a large brush.

Plastic Wood: A tube of plastic wood in natural color is easiest to use. It is squeezed from the tube and applied directly onto wood surfaces or squeezed out in small amounts and applied with a toothpick. Always squeeze tube gently and remember to replace cap to keep wood from drying out.

Tools: A small saw, tack hammer, and a round file are common to most households. If not found in Mother's tool box, they will be found among your father's tools. Always return tools when you have finished using them.

Take care whenever using saws, scissors, or pointed objects. Don't try to cut out tiny pieces with large shears when a small pair of scissors will do a better job. When using sharp tools, such as saws, cut carefully and always cut away from yourself.

Starting a Project

1. Read through the list of materials first.
2. Gather together all the materials and tools needed.
3. Read through the directions and fit the pieces together.
4. Prepare your work area.

When you follow this procedure, small problems can be solved and changes made before you begin working. For instance, the dowel which fits into a spool hole but is just a little too large for the bead can be made thinner by sanding the part which will be inside the bead with sandpaper. If the bead hole is extremely small, then another bead will have to be substituted.

If you find you do not have a particular material required, the time to find a substitute is before you start to work. A small spool can often be used for a head instead of a large bead. A square block of wood will take the place of a drawer pull base if you make the pincushion lady (page 113), and a man's handkerchief can be substituted for the parachute of the sky diver (page 24).

Many materials can be used in place of others. Use your imagination and you'll develop new ideas; that's the wonderful part of creating things. It's a way of expressing yourself, your ideas, your favorite colors, in the things you make.

Cover your work area—a table, desk, or workbench—with many layers of newspaper to protect the top from scratches and to make cleaning up easier. It is much simpler to wrap up and discard newspaper than to clean paint or glue off a table.

Cleaning Up

Whatever paint you use, be sure to clean the brushes immediately after you finish painting. When you use gesso or any type of poster paint, clean the brushes with soap and water. If you use enamels, pour a little turpentine in a small glass jar, swish your brush around until all paint is removed, then wash the brush with soap and warm water.

Before putting lids on paint jars, wipe the rims with a damp cloth to remove paint and to prevent lids from sticking. Then be sure to screw lids on tightly.

Mothers enjoy watching their children create and make things, but they do not enjoy cleaning up after them. So, do be neat as you work and put all your materials and tools away and clean up immediately after you have finished.

Working Techniques

1. *Spools:* Peel paper labels from spools. Then with warm water and gentle rubbing with a finger, remove any paper still sticking to the wood. Do not place or soak spools in water; they will warp. If paper is hard to remove, sand lightly with fine sandpaper.

2. *Gluing:* Too little or too much glue will result in an item falling apart or a messy looking project. When you glue spools together, apply the glue evenly over the surfaces with a small brush and immediately press them together. If the pieces slide against each other, wait a few seconds, then press them together again. Wipe off excess glue with a damp cloth. A small, wet brush is also handy for removing excess glue from places which are difficult to reach with a damp cloth.

Only a very thin layer of white, liquid glue, spread evenly, is needed for sticking felt or fabric. Too much glue will make fabric stiff and messy.

14

When you glue two pieces of cardboard together, it's best to press them until dry under a heavy book so they will be flat.

3. *Painting:* Spools and new wood soak up paint. Therefore, the wood *must* be sealed before paint is applied. Clear shellac can be used but gesso is better. For a nice smooth finish, paint wood with two thin coats of gesso, letting the first coat dry before applying the second. Slippery, smooth or waxy surfaces often cause poster paints to "crawl" and they won't stay on properly. Sometimes the addition of liquid soap to the paint will help, but if two coats of gesso are painted on such surfaces, you will have no trouble making poster paint stick.

Before beginning to paint, mix the paints well, stirring gently with clean sticks. Air bubbles will result if you stir too fast and you will have to wait until the paint settles and bubbles disappear or your painted surfaces will be filled with tiny holes. Sometimes your project will need two coats of paint to ensure a bright, well-covered surface. But don't forget to let each coat dry thoroughly before putting on the next coat. Although poster paints dry quickly and the surface may seem dry, it is wise to give them a little extra drying time to avoid smearing or blurring. Also, don't load your brushes with too much paint. Dip the bristles in and remove excess paint by lightly pressing the bristles against the edge of the jar. Then apply paint to the surface, using short even strokes all going in one direction. Apply a clear fixative after paint is completely dry.

4. *Dowel Sticks:* When the directions tell you to use a ¼ inch in diameter dowel (the size used for most spool projects) but the one you have is just a little too round, enlarge the hole with a round file until the dowel fits. Don't try to enlarge a hole to fit a dowel the size of a broom handle, it just won't work! If, on the other hand, your dowel stick is a bit smaller than the hole, this can be fixed by gluing a strip of paper around the portion of stick which will be inside the spool or spools. But don't glue too much paper around the stick or you'll make the dowel so fat it won't fit.

5. *Plastic Wood:* When first squeezed from the tube and applied to wood surfaces, plastic wood is moist and sticky. Therefore, do not try to shape or mold it until the surface begins to dry and is no longer tacky. Use toothpicks for applying, shaping, and molding, but change to a clean one when ends become covered with sticky wood. Toothpicks can be used again if you wipe off sticky wood with a cloth or scrape away dried wood with a fingernail.

Always apply plastic wood one layer at a time. Let the wood dry until it is completely hard before putting on the next layer. Although plastic wood dries quickly, you will find it does not dry so fast that you cannot remove it if you make a mistake. You will also find that you will have plenty of time to mold and shape the wood before it becomes hard. Once hard, plastic wood can be sanded if a smooth surface is desired.

6. Sawing: Soft woods, such as balsa, pine, and basswood, are easy to cut. Spools, which are made of hardwood, require a bit of patience when sawing. Always mark wood or spool with pencil and follow pencil line as you saw to ensure a straight cut. Use a vise to hold wood as you saw. Let the saw work for you; don't try to push it through the wood. Use slight pressure on the forward cut, easy on the backward cut.

7. Sanding and Filing: All edges cut with a saw and rough surfaces must be sanded to give your project a finished look. Small pieces of sandpaper, cut from larger sheets and wrapped around a small block of wood, are easier to use. Begin sanding with a medium grade sandpaper and, as the surface becomes smooth, change to a finer grade. Continue sanding until area is flat, smooth, and even. Emery boards, the same kind Mother uses for her nails, are excellent for smoothing small pieces and the thin edges of both wood and cardboard.

A round file is used to enlarge the inside spool hole whenever required. Work evenly around the inside hole, using a back-and-forth and circular motion.

8. Measuring: Never guess at measurements, always use a ruler or yardstick. Measure correctly and mark with pencil.

9. *Using a Compass:* Use a compass to draw circles. Directions will tell you the radius to set your compass for the correct size circle needed.

If you need to puncture a hole in cardboard or paper where a paper punch will not reach, use a compass point. Protect the working surface with an old magazine first, lay the cardboard on top, then press and turn the compass point in the spot where a hole is needed.

10. *Tracing and Transferring Patterns:* To trace patterns, lay a piece of tracing or white tissue paper over the illustration. Hold it in place with paper clips. Use a soft pencil for tracing and a ruler for straight edges. Draw over all lines, details, and markings carefully.

To transfer pattern, use carbon paper. Place it shiny side down on whatever material the directions tell you, then put the tracing on top. Hold them all in place with masking tape. Draw over all lines of the tracing again with a hard pencil to transfer the pattern. Be sure you have drawn on all lines before removing the tracing.

Another way to transfer a pattern is to scribble all over the back of the tracing with the side of a soft pencil point until the paper is evenly covered with pencil carbon. Lay the tracing on the material called for, with the scribbled side down, and draw over the tracing again to transfer.

11. *Sewing:* Size 50 cotton or mercerized thread in colors to match fabric is used for all sewing unless directions suggest a contrasting color or different type thread. Sew with the smallest size needle you can use most comfortably, with an eye large enough to be threaded easily. Crewel needles have long eyes and are easy to thread, and an assortment of embroidery needles will provide you with the right size needle for each project.

The stitches you will be using for sewing are the running stitch and the gathering stitch. (See illustrations, page 18.)

Always fasten thread securely at the end of sewing by making three tiny backstitches one on top of the other (see illustration). To do this, first make a tiny running stitch, then push the point of the needle in the beginning of the running stitch and out the end. Do this again to make three stitches, one on top of the other.

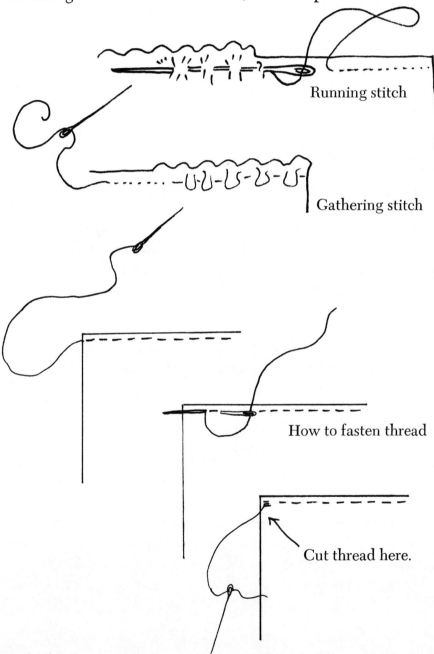

Running stitch

Gathering stitch

How to fasten thread

Cut thread here.

Spool People

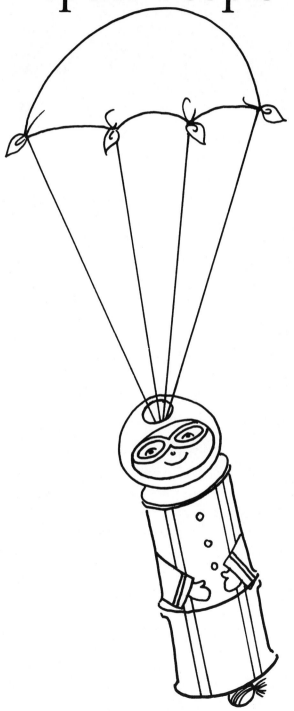

Little People

You Will Need:
>small spools
>large round wooden beads
>small plastic bottle caps (saved from
empty bottles and tubes, such as tooth-
paste and baby aspirin)
>glue, paints, brushes

How to Make It:
All the little people are made alike. You
can make them look different by painting
their hair and bodies different colors and
by giving them different smiles and features. Some can wear small bottle caps for
hats.

1. Put some glue around one spool hole
and around one bead hole. Push the glued
parts together (Step 2, Working Techniques). The bead will be the head and
the spool will be the body. If your little
figure is to wear a hat, glue a bottle cap on
the head.

2. Paint the spool and hat a solid color
and the head a skin color, and let dry.
Then paint features on face, hair on head,
and buttons, a collar or a belt on the body.
The illustrations suggest ways of painting
the little people, but use your own ideas
too. Now, make more little people, make
a whole townful. Make four little people
for the pegboard shown on page 21 and
give it to your little brother or sister or
friend.

Little People Pegboard

You Will Need:

4 short spools, the size used for silk thread (or saw 2 small spools in half cross-wise)

4 tiny spools (the size found in mending kits)

a piece of wood, 9 inches long, 3 inches wide, and about ½ inch thick

a piece of dowel stick, 7 inches long and ¼ inch in diameter (to fit snugly into tiny spool holes)

small saw, sandpaper, glue, pencil, ruler, paints, brushes

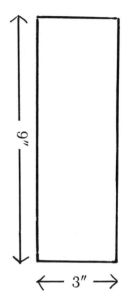

9"

← 3" →

How to Make It:

1. Sand the piece of wood until it is nice and smooth (Step 7, Working Techniques). Lay the wood flat on your working surface. Glue a short spool to each corner of the board. These spools will be the pegboard's feet. Let glue dry, then turn board over.

2. Stand four little people on the board. Arrange them any way you wish. When you decide where the little people should stand, pick them up, one by one, and make a pencil dot right where they stood. Put the little people aside until you've finished the pegboard. Next, spread glue on one end of a tiny spool and stick it right on top of a pencil mark. Do the same thing with the other three tiny spools.

3. Measure and mark the dowel stick into four 1¾-inch pieces. Saw the stick into four pieces. These four pieces of dowel will be pegs. Sand the cut edges of each until smooth. Put glue all over one end of a peg and push it into one of the tiny spools. Do the same thing with the other three dowel pieces so that each tiny spool has a peg sticking out of it.

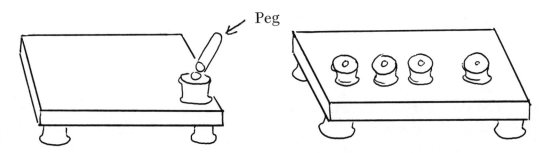

Peg

4. Paint the board a solid color. Paint the tiny spools a skin color so they will look like legs when the little people stand on the pegs. Paint one peg a solid color to match the body of one little person. Make another peg the color of another little person. Do the same thing with the other two pegs, then let dry. Now your friend, brother, or sister can match colors and have fun standing their little friends on the pegboard.

Little People Seesaw

You Will Need:

a large spool

piece of thin wood, 8 inches long, about 1¼ inches wide and ⅛ inch thick (a piece of old yardstick will be perfect)

2 brads (skinny nails), about ⅝ inch long

2 plastic bottle caps, the kind found on plastic aspirin bottles (caps must be deep enough for little people to sit in)

tack hammer

glue, paints, brushes

How to Make It:

1. Lay the middle of the wood piece on the side of the large spool. Hammer the two brads all the way through wood and into the spool. Place the brads side by side across the wood piece. Turn the caps upside down. Glue one to each end of the wood piece.

2. Paint seesaw. Paint the bottle cap seats another color. Let dry. Put one of the little people in one seat and another in the other seat.

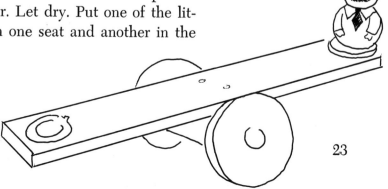

Scarf

Sky Diver

You Will Need:

1 medium spool

1 small spool

1 large wooden bead (from a baby's bead-stringing set)

1 small bead (larger than hole in small spool)

strong black thread (called carpet and button thread)

a 16 x 16 inch square silk scarf or a man's handkerchief

thin dowel stick, glue, paints, brushes, scissors, ruler, big sewing needle with a large eye

How to Make It:

1. Glue the two spools one on top of the other, then glue the large bead head on the medium spool. The small spool will be the sky diver's legs and the medium spool his body. Carefully push the thin dowel through the spools and bead to make sure the glue has not covered the holes.

2. Paint the spools a solid color, the head bead a skin color and the small bead the same color as the spools. Let dry, then paint features on face, arms, and some jump-suit detail on body (see illustration). Paint a bright yellow helmet on the bead head.

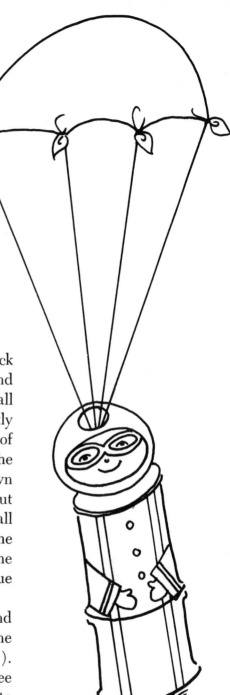

3. Cut four 15-inch pieces of strong black thread. Put all the threads together and push them through the hole in the small bead. Knot and tie the thread tightly around the bead. Hold the other ends of threads together and push them into the large-eyed needle. Drop the needle down through the spool body until it comes out the top of the head. Put glue on the small bead. Pull the threads at the top of the head until the bead fits tightly against the spool hole. Hold the threads until the glue dries and the bead stays in place.

4. Separate the four threads. Then tie and knot one end of a thread tightly to one corner of the silk scarf (the parachute). Do the same thing with the other three threads, so that you have a thread tied to each corner of the scarf. Now toss your sky diver high into the air. He will float and soar all the way to the ground.

Robot

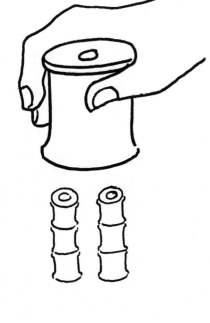

You Will Need:
> 1 large spool
> 1 small spool
> 7 tiny spools (the size found in mending kits)
> cardboard
> paints: silver, black, white, and red
> 2 thumbtacks
> 7-inch piece of thin, flexible wire
> a piece of thin dowel stick (smaller than tiny spool hole)
> tracing paper
> glue, pencil, scissors, brushes

How to Make It:

1. Glue three tiny spools one on top of the other. Do the same with three other tiny spools. These will be the robot's legs. Stand the legs side by side and glue the large spool body on top of them. Glue the small spool head on the body and the last tiny spool on top of the head.

2. Trace the patterns of foot and arm onto tracing paper and transfer them to cardboard (Step 10, Working Techniques). Make two feet and two arms, then cut them out.

3. Glue a foot to the bottom of each leg. Fold back the tab of each arm and brush glue on the tabs, then stick an arm to each side of body.

4. Wind the piece of wire around the thin

stick. Slide the wire off the stick and push one end into the tiny spool on top of the head. It will look like a spring.

5. Paint the robot with silver paint. Let dry. Paint square black eyes and a red rectangular mouth on the face spool. Paint a white square for panelboard on front of the body spool and let dry. Paint a small black rectangle on the white panelboard. All robots have dials. When paint is dry, push the thumbtacks into the panelboard for knobs to turn the dials.

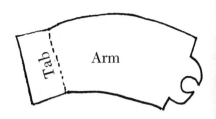

Castle Guard

Spear

You Will Need:
>2 medium spools
>1 small spool
>a large wheel or tire-shaped bead (from a baby's bead-stringing set)
>a tube of plastic wood
>small saw
>2 Popsicle sticks
>1 tall plastic bottle cap
>1 small bead with large hole
>6-inch piece of thin dowel stick, thin enough to fit into small bead
>a small feather
>toothpicks, glue, sandpaper, paints, brushes

How to Make It:
1. Glue a medium spool, wheel bead, and the other medium spool together, one on top of the other with the bead between the two spools. Glue the small spool head on one of the medium spools.
2. Squeeze small dabs of plastic wood from the tube (Step 5, Working Techniques) and, using a toothpick, apply them to the spool head, shaping and building up a long-hair style like the one in the illustration. Push the tall bottle cap hat on the head while the wood is still wet. Let the hair dry. Next put a tiny ball of plastic wood on the face and shape it into a nose. When dry, add more wood on the face for a mustache and beard. Let dry.

28

3. Saw a Popsicle stick in half to make two pieces. These will be the guard's arms. With sandpaper, round off the cut ends of each stick. Now, glue an arm to each side of the spool body. Hold them in place until glue dries.

4. Saw a 1-inch piece off the other Popsicle stick. With sandpaper, shape the piece into a spear blade (see illustration). Put glue on the square end of the blade and push it into the small bead. Let dry. Then brush glue on one end of the piece of thin dowel stick and push it into the bead hole from the other side.

5. Paint the castle guard, using your favorite colors. You could paint the spear handle brown and the blade gray or silver. Let dry.

6. Stand the spear in position, placing it against the guard's arm. Put glue on the stick and the arm where they touch each other and on the bottom of the stick where it touches the bottom spool. Stand the spear in place again and hold it there until the glue dries. Finally, glue the small feather to front of hat.

Dolls
and Doll Furniture

China Doll

You Will Need:

1 large spool (with rim larger in diameter than the extra-large bead head)

1 medium spool

1 small spool

an extra-large round bead about 1 inch in diameter (from a baby's bead-stringing set)

a small bead, a little larger than large spool hole

small saw

sandpaper, glue, paints, brushes

How to Make It:

1. Saw one rim off the large spool. (See Steps 6 and 7, Working Techniques.) Sand cut edges of both the spool and the rim until smooth and flat. The rim slice will be a hat; put it aside until later.

2. Glue the medium spool on the cut edge of the large spool. Then glue the small spool on the medium one. These three spools will be the doll's body. Next, glue the extra-large bead head on the body, sticking it to the small spool. Now, spread glue on the cut side of that sawed-off rim and stick it flat on top of the bead head. Finally, glue the small bead on the hat over the hole.

3. Paint the spool body blue, the head a skin color, and the hat red. Let dry. Then

paint facial features and hair on head and a red-flowered design on the body. (See illustration.) Let paint dry. Finally paint hat, ties and a tiny bow under doll's chin over the hair and face color.

Rim cut from spool

South American Fruit Seller

You Will Need:
 1 small spool
 1 large spool
 extra-large round bead with large hole (from a baby's bead-stringing set)
 a small wood drawer pull (or saw another large spool in half and use one piece in place of drawer pull)
 large saucer-shaped coat button
 small beads, in assorted shapes
 a piece of dowel stick, 1 inch long and ¼ inch in diameter
 glue, sandpaper, paints, brushes

How to Make It:
1. Turn drawer pull upside down on a flat surface. If it rocks, sand the rounded side with sandpaper until it sits flat. Turn drawer pull upside down again and glue the large spool on top. Then glue the small spool on the large one. This will be the doll's body. Brush glue on one end of the piece of dowel stick. Push it into small spool, letting ¾ inch extend above the top of spool. Put glue on the other end of stick and push the extra-large bead head on top. Let some of the stick show for neck.
2. Make a fruit basket from the large button. Brush glue on one side of small beads and stick them on the button. Arrange beads to look like fruits. A group of tiny

beads could be grapes, small round beads can be oranges, and oval beads look like bananas and melons. You may need to use a pair of tweezers to hold and place the beads in the basket. When basket is filled, glue it on the large bead head.

3. Paint the spool body a bright color and the neck and head a skin color. Make the basket brown. Let paint dry, then put facial features and hair on head and a wide sash and dots on the dress. When paint has dried, use a tiny brush to paint the bead fruit solid colors. Let dry, then put some detail on the fruit—brown spots, rosy-red cheeks, green stems.

Clown Doll

You Will Need:

    2 small spools

    2 short spools, the size used for silk thread; or saw a small spool in half crosswise

    2 large spools

    scraps of felt, in assorted colors

    piece of cotton fringe, about 4 inches long (called moss fringe)

    a cotton pompon (cut off a leftover piece of ball fringe)

    sewing needle with large eye

    elastic cord

    tracing paper, pencil, straight pins, scissors, glue, paints, brushes

Hand

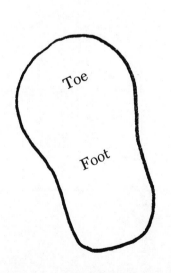

Toe

Foot

How to Make It:

1. Paint all spools. Make the small spools and the short spools yellow, one of the large spools green, and the other large spool white. Let dry. Then paint facial features on the white spool, the clown's head. When dry, glue the cotton fringe around the top rim of the spool head for hair.

2. Trace the patterns for hand and foot onto tracing paper. Cut them out. Pin patterns on felt and cut out four hands and four feet. Glue two feet together, then glue two hands together. Do the same thing with the other hands and feet. This will give you two feet and two hands made of a double thickness of felt.

3. Now trace the two flower patterns and cut them out. Pin flowers to felt and cut out felt in the same shape. Using the large flower pattern, cut out six different-colored flowers. Then, using the small flower pattern, cut out eighty-three felt flowers. Make them as many different colors as you can. You can cut two layers of felt at one time. Instead of making the clown's costume of flower shapes, try circles or stars or use an idea of your own.

4. With scissors, cut a piece of elastic cord about 12 inches long. Thread it into the large-eyed needle and make a big knot in one end. Next, string doll together. Push the needle through one foot, where the dot is on the pattern, and into a small yellow spool. Then, one at a time, push needle through the center of twenty-five small felt flowers. This will be one of the clown's legs. Now take needle into large green body spool and through the center of three large felt flowers (these will be the collar) and into the spool head. The hat comes next; so push the needle through the cen-

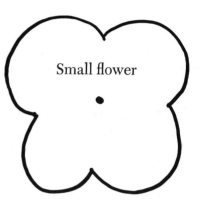

Small flower

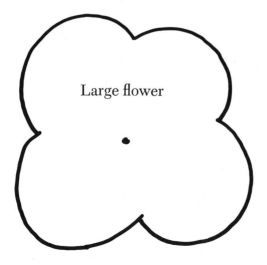

Large flower

ter of three more large flowers and three small flowers. Remove needle from cord. Cut another piece of elastic cord 12 inches long. String the other leg exactly as you did before. Then push the needle through the body spool, the center of the collar flowers, into the head spool and through the hat flowers. Remove the needle. Hold the two elastic pieces together. Pull them gently until both legs are the same length, but don't pull the elastic too tight. Tie the two pieces of elastic together just above the hat. Tie several knots to make sure the cords won't come apart.

5. To give your doll arms, first cut a piece of elastic cord about 16 inches long and thread it in the needle. Put the two ends together and make a big knot. Then, push the needle through a hand near the straight edge, where the dot is on the pattern, and into one of the short spools. Next string on fifteen small felt flowers just as you did for the legs. Now pull the head and body spools apart underneath the collar. Push the needle through between the two cords used for the body. String on fifteen more flowers for the other arm and the other short spool. Finally add the hand. Pull the cord gently to adjust the arms and tie a knot in the cord right at the hand. Tie another knot on top of the first one. Cut off excess cord. Glue the pompon to the top of the hat to hide the knot. Your clown doll is finished.

Dollhouse Doll

You Will Need:

a tiny spool, the size found in mending kits

18 inches of narrow pink cotton tubing (available at fabric shops)

pink sewing thread

sewing needle

2 pipe cleaners or chenille stems, one 12 inches long and the other 4 inches long

piece of felt for dress, 6 inches long and 3 inches wide

sewing thread to match felt

scrap of felt in another color

small amount of knitting yarn, in a hair color

scissors, paints, brushes, glue, ruler, tracing paper, pencil, straight pins

How to Make It:

1. Paint the tiny spool a skin color, and let dry. Then paint on facial features. This will be doll's head.

2. With scissors, cut a 6-inch piece of cotton tubing for doll's arms. The remaining 12 inches of tubing will be the body. Inside the body is a piece of cord; pull it out. Just hold the cord and push the tubing back until string is removed. Then, push the 12-inch pipe cleaner inside the tubing. Bend the body in half to make a skinny U-shape. The curved part will be the neck. Next, remove the cord from inside the arm

piece and push the 4-inch length of pipe cleaner inside. Each end of the cotton tubing should extend 1 inch beyond the pipe cleaner. Tie each end into a knot to make hands. Now lay the middle of the arm piece across the body about 1 inch down from the curved end. Thread needle with pink thread and sew the arms to the body, using small running stitches. Put glue on the top of the curved end and push it into the spool head. Let a little of the tubing show for the doll's neck.

3. For shoes, trace the shoe pattern onto tracing paper (Step 10, Working Techniques). Pin pattern on the scrap of felt and cut out four shoes. Brush glue on one side of a felt shoe, then stick the end of a leg on top. Finally, put another shoe on top of the leg. Press them all together with your fingers. You will have two shoe shapes glued together with the end of the leg between. Attach a shoe to the other leg end in the same way. When glue has dried, bend shoes up.

4. To give doll hair, cut knitting yarn into eight 6-inch pieces. Put glue on the spool head and lay the middle of each yarn strand across the top of the head on the wet glue. Let dry. Using sewing thread (the same color as the dress), tie the yarn strands together at each side of face. Trim yarn ends so that they are all even.

5. Trace dress pattern onto tracing paper. Pin pattern onto felt and cut out two pieces in the same shape. Put the two felt

Shoe

dresses together, one on top of the other. Thread the needle with matching thread and starting at point marked A on the pattern, sew the underarm seam together to point marked B. The running stitches should be small and kept as close to the edge as you can. Sew the other underarm seam in the same way. Turn the dress inside out, so the stitches are on the inside.

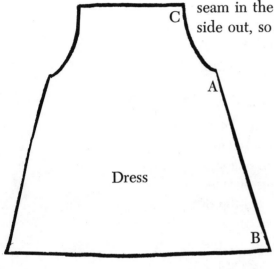

Dress

Put the dress on the doll and gather the neck edge to fit. Start at point marked C on the pattern and sew running stitches across the front of the dress from one shoulder to the other. When you get to the end, push the needle through to the back shoulder, then sew across the back neck edge. Finally, push the needle through to where you started at point C. Pull thread to gather neck and fasten thread securely (Step 11, Working Techniques). Now bend the doll into a sitting position. She is just the right size to sit or lounge on the patio furniture in this book.

Make a whole family of dolls in the same way. A boy doll can wear a jacket. (Use the jacket pattern for monkey on page 44.) Cut two pants from felt (see illustration) and sew together. Gather waist of pants to fit doll's waist. For hair, cut some yarn into a pile of tiny pieces. Apply glue to top of spool head and dip head into yarn.

Mother and Father dolls should be taller; just make their legs about 1 inch longer than legs of girl doll. Use the girl's dress pattern for the mother but make it a little longer. Also increase the length of legs when making pants for Father.

1"

Pants

2"

Monkey Doll

You Will Need:

 1 tiny spool, the size found in mending kits
 a piece of narrow brown cotton tubing, 17 inches long
 2 brown pipe cleaners, 12 inches long
 small piece of felt fabric, about 4 inches long and 3 inches
wide
 scrap of brown felt
 matching sewing threads
 sewing needle
 straight pins
 6-inch piece of narrow ribbon
 a 25-cent piece, or something circular, about 1 inch in
diameter
 chalk, ruler, scissors, tracing paper, pencil, glue, paints,
brushes, paper punch

How to Make It:

1. Paint the tiny spool brown and let dry. Then paint on a light-

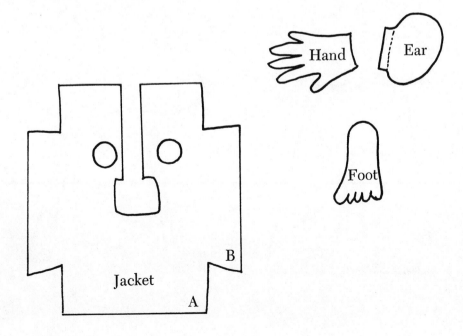

brown mask for face. When paint has dried, put on facial features.
2. With scissors, cut a 4-inch length of brown cotton tubing. This
will be the monkey's arms. Cut another 4-inch piece and save it
for the tail. The remaining 8 inches of tubing will be the body.
Inside the body tubing is a cord; pull it out. Cut an 8-inch length
of pipe cleaner and push it inside the tubing. Bend the body tubing in half. The curved part will be the neck. Pull the cord out of
the arm tubing. Cut a 4-inch piece of pipe cleaner and push it
inside the arms. Now lay the middle of the arms across the body
½ inch below the neck. Thread needle with brown thread and
sew arms to body, using small running stitches. Remove the cord
from the tail tubing. Tie a knot in one end, then push a 3-inch
piece of pipe cleaner into the other end. Sew the end without the
knot to the body 1 inch below arms. Next, put glue on top of neck
and push it into spool head. Let some of the tubing show for
neck.
3. Trace patterns for hands, feet, and ears onto tracing paper
(Step 10, Working Techniques). Pin the patterns onto brown felt
and cut out four hands, four feet, and two ears. Brush glue on
both ear tabs and stick an ear to each side of head. Put glue on
one side of a felt hand. Stick it to the end of one arm, then stick another hand to the other side of the arm. Press them together with
your fingers. You will have two felt hands glued together with an
arm end between. Attach the other hands to the other arm and
the feet to the leg ends in the same way.
4. Trace pattern for jacket onto tracing paper. Pin pattern to felt
and cut out one felt shape. Using paper punch, punch a hole in
each jacket front where shown on pattern. Fold the jacket fronts
down, matching the front and back underarm edges. Thread
needle with thread to match the felt and, starting at point A and
ending at point B, sew underarm seam together, using running
stitches. Sew the other underarm seam in the same way. Put jacket
on monkey. Push narrow ribbon through both holes in jacket front,
then tie ribbon in a bow.

5. Put the 25-cent piece on top of a piece of felt and trace around it with chalk to make a circle. Cut it out, then brush glue on top of monkey's head and stick felt circle on top for hat. Now make the rocking horse (see next project). Then bend the monkey into a sitting position, put him on the horse, and give him a ride!

Rocking Horse

You Will Need:
> 1 large spool
> cardboard
> small amount of red and black knitting yarn
> piece of very narrow ribbon or braid, about 6 inches long
> tracing paper
> 2 small sequins
> pencil, glue, paints, brushes, scissors

How to Make It:
1. Trace the patterns for head and rockers onto the tracing paper and transfer to cardboard. Draw two heads and four rockers. Cut them out with scissors.
2. Glue two rockers together (Step 2, Working Techniques). Do the same with the other two. Spread glue on one horse head up to the dotted line of the tab. Don't glue the tabs together because they will be used to attach the head to the spool body. Lay the other head on top, then spread the tabs open, in opposite directions. Put some glue on point marked A in the illustration of head pattern and on the bottom of the tabs. Push point A into the spool hole and press tabs onto the body. Glue a rocker to each side of the body. Hold the spool body and stand the horse on a table to be sure both rockers are on straight and the horse stands evenly.
3. Paint the body and rockers red, the head white and let dry. Use black paint to outline mouth, nose, mane, ears, and eyes, on both sides of the head. Put spots on the body and let dry.
4. Cut the yarn into five pieces, each 6 inches long. Put all the pieces together and make a knot right in the middle of all the strands. This will be your horse's tail. Put glue on the knot and push it into the spool hole at back of body. Trim the yarn ends

evenly. Fold the narrow ribbon in half and put the center right over the edge of the horse's nose, then glue the ribbon to both sides of the head. Knot the ends of the ribbon together for the reins. Glue a sequin on the reins, at each side of the head.

Tab

A

Rocker

Dollhouse Lamp

You Will Need:

    1 small spool

    dowel stick, 3 inches long and ¼ inch in diameter

    plastic bottle cap, about 1¼ inches high and 1¼ inches in diameter

    thumbtack

    glue, paints, brushes, tack hammer

How to Make It:

1. Put glue around one end of the dowel stick and push it into the spool.

2. Paint the spool lamp base and stick a solid color and let dry.

3. When the solid color has dried, paint a flower design on the spool.

4. Put the bottle cap on the stick; this will be the lamp shade. Put the thumbtack in the top center of the bottle cap. Hammer the thumbtack lightly until it goes through the cap and into the stick.

Dollhouse Patio Set

You Will Need:
    1 large spool
    2 small spools
    a plastic coffee can lid, about 4 inches in diameter
    small piece of cardboard
    small piece of felt and scraps of another color
    dowel stick, about 6 inches long and ¼ inch in diameter
    construction paper
    compass
    paper punch
    paints, brushes, glue, pencil, scissors

How to Make It:
1. Put a small spool on top of the cardboard and trace around it with pencil. Do this twice to make two circles. Cut out the circles with scissors.
2. Glue a cardboard circle on top of each small spool. These are the stools; the large spool will be the table base. With the point of your compass, make a small hole in the center of the plastic coffee can lid (Step 9, Working Techniques). Glue lid to the top of the large spool, matching holes. Put glue around one end of the dowel stick and push it down through the center of the plastic lid and into the spool.
3. Paint the table, umbrella stick, and stools a solid color (Step 3, Working Techniques), and let dry.

4. Set the compass at a ¾-inch radius and draw two circles on the felt. Cut them out and glue one to the top of one stool, over the cardboard circle, and the other circle to the top of the other stool.

5. Set the compass at a 3-inch radius and draw a circle on the construction paper. Cut it out and glue it to a felt piece. Cut out a felt circle. This will be the umbrella. Slit the circle from one edge to the center (see illustration). Then pull one slit edge over the other, until the circle forms an open umbrella shape, and glue together along the straight edges. Snip a tiny hole from the center of the circle.

6. Put glue around the umbrella stick about ½ inch from the top, and more glue on the inside of the umbrella around the center hole. Push the stick through the hole, letting a little of the stick show at the top, and pinch the umbrella around the stick. With the paper punch, punch out some dots from the felt scraps. Glue them on the umbrella and stool covers.

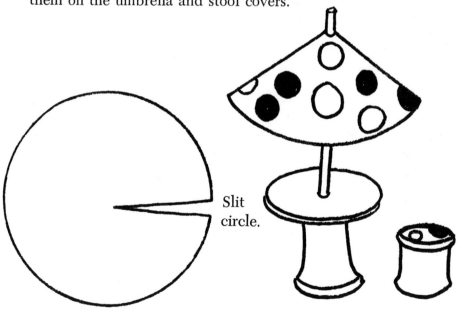

Slit circle.

Patio Chair

You Will Need:

1 small spool

a plastic basket, 8 inches long and 2½ inches wide (the kind that often holds tomatoes) or substitute a long, narrow cardboard box of about the same size (from candy or cheese)

small piece of felt and scraps of another color (same colors as patio set if you like)

sewing thread to match felt

sewing needle

cotton batting or absorbent cotton

ruler, scissors, glue, paper punch, paints, brushes

How to Make It:

1. Tomato baskets come in different designs, but they are all about the same size. Cut your basket as shown in the illustration. Measure 2 inches from one end of basket and cut it apart right after the first thin side bar. This will make the chair. Save the remaining part of basket to make the chaise lounge.

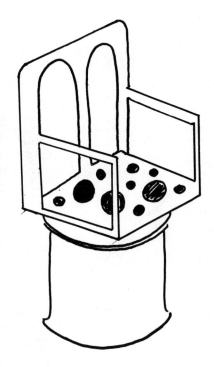

2. Glue the chair on top of the small spool, placing spool right under the circle design in basket bottom. Paint chair to match patio set, and let dry.

3. To make the seat cushion, cut two squares from felt, each 2 x 2 inches, then put them together, one on top of the other. Thread needle with matching thread and sew squares together along three sides, using a running stitch. Make stitches small and close to edge. Stuff pillow with cotton batting or absorbent cotton and sew fourth side closed. Punch some dots from felt scraps with paper punch and glue on cushion to match patio umbrella. Put cushion in chair.

If using a cardboard box, cut it in the same way as basket. Then cut out sides to make arms (see illustration). Save the remaining part of box to make the chaise lounge.

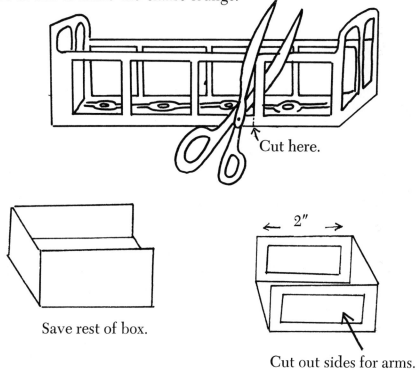

Cut here.

Save rest of box.

2"

Cut out sides for arms.

Patio Chaise Lounge

You Will Need:

    2 small spools
    plastic tomato basket (the part left over from patio chair)
    small piece of felt fabric and scraps of another color
    sewing thread to match felt
    sewing needle
    cotton batting or absorbent cotton
    ruler, scissors, glue, paper punch, paints, brushes

How to Make It:

1. Use the part of basket saved from patio chair to make chaise lounge. Measure 4 inches from uncut end and cut across basket. Then cut arms right after first thin bar, just like the chair, but leave a long seat. Discard leftover pieces of basket.

2. Glue a small spool under one circle design in basket bottom. Then put other spool under the other circle. Paint chaise lounge to match patio chair, and let dry.

3. To make seat cushion, cut two rectangular pieces from felt, both 4 inches long and 2 inches wide. Put them together, one on top of the other. With matching thread sew three sides of cushion together, using small running stitches. Keep stitches close to edge. Stuff pillow with cotton batting or absorbent cotton, then sew fourth side closed. With a paper punch, punch some dots from felt scraps. Glue them on the cushion, then put it on chaise lounge.

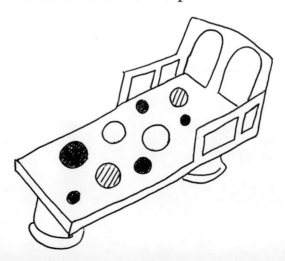

Desk and Chair

You Will Need:
- 4 small spools
- 1 small fat spool
- 3 small empty matchboxes
- 3 small round beads
- 2 rectangular pieces of cardboard, each 4½ inches long and 2½ inches wide
- a circular wooden button about 1¼ inches in diameter
- small piece of cardboard
- pencil, sandpaper, scissors, paints, brushes

How to Make It:

1. Make the desk first. Glue the three matchboxes side by side, flat on one cardboard rectangle. Place the boxes so that some of the cardboard shows all around them. Next brush glue all over the top of the three matchboxes and stick on the other cardboard rectangle. Be sure to place it so that all sides are exactly even with the

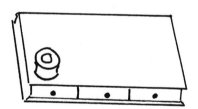

Sand paper

bottom cardboard. Press the top cardboard with your hand to keep everything flat until the glue dries. The matchboxes will be the drawers, one cardboard piece will be the top, and the other cardboard will be the underside of the desk. To make drawer pulls, put a small dab of glue on one end of a drawer and stick on a bead. Do the same thing with the other drawers and beads. Now brush glue on one end of a small spool and paste it underneath one corner of the cardboard. (Slide open a drawer to see which cardboard rectangle is the underside piece.) Glue a small spool in each of the other three corners. Let dry, then stand desk on its spool legs.

2. Now make the chair. Put the small fat spool on top of cardboard and trace around it with pencil to make a circle. Cut out circle with scissors and glue it to one end of the fat spool. Next rub one side edge of the button with sandpaper until the edge is flat and straight. The button will be the chair back. Put glue on the flattened part and stick it on top of the cardboard covered spool, matching the back edge of the button with the edge of the cardboard circle.

3. Remove the drawers from desk. Paint the desk and the drawer fronts and backs a solid color, and let dry. Don't paint the *sides* of matchbox drawers; that may make them fit too tight. Paint the chair to match desk. When paint has dried, slide drawers in place.

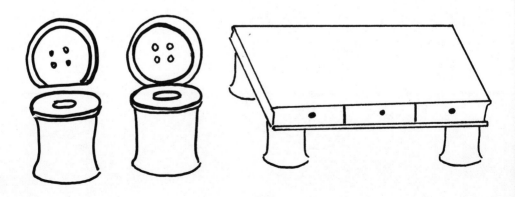

Spool Toys

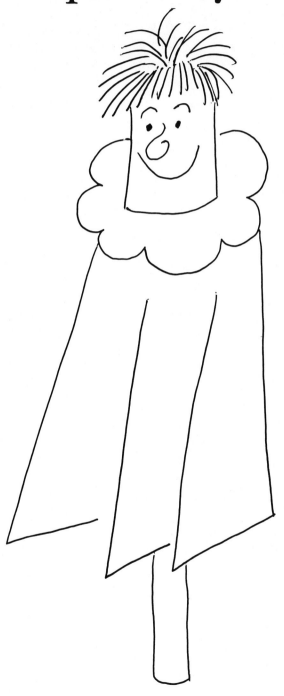

Spiral-Go-Round

You Will Need:

    1 large spool

    new, just sharpened pencil (it should fit tightly into spool hole)

    circular piece of cardboard, about 2 inches in diameter

    small piece of bright-colored construction paper

    compass

    scissors, pencil, paints, brushes, glue

How to Make It:

1. Glue the spool to the center of the cardboard circle. This will be the base.
2. Paint base and let dry.
3. Set the compass at a 1½-inch radius and draw a circle on the construction paper. Don'ᴛ make a hole with the compass point. There should be a slight indentation in the center of the paper circle—not a hole. Cut out paper circle, then cut it into a spiral. Begin cutting on the opposite side of the depression made by the point of the

Cut circle into a spiral.

compass and cut around and around in a continuous circle from the outer edge almost to the center (see illustration). Leave a whole circle in the center.

4. Push the pencil down into the spool hole with the point sticking up. Place the center of the spiral on the pencil, with the point resting in the depression. Place your spiral-go-round over a lighted electric bulb (set it on the finial of a lamp if it has a flat top), on a radiator, near a hot-air register or on a stack of books above and close to a baseboard radiator. The rising hot air will make the spiral-go-round spin.

Pink Pig

You Will Need:
1 large spool
4 tiny bottle corks, ½ inch high
1 small bottle cork, ¾ inch high
piece of pink pipe cleaner, about 3 inches long
scrap of lightweight cardboard
scissors, glue, paints, brushes, tracing paper, pencil

How to Make It:
1. Glue the small ¾-inch cork to one end of spool. This will be pig's snout. For legs, glue the tiny corks to body of spool. The corks should tilt slightly outward. Stand pig on its legs before glue dries to be sure it stands evenly.

2. Trace pattern for ear onto tracing paper and transfer it to cardboard. Cut out two ear shapes. Put glue on bottom edge of each ear and stick them to back of spool rim at top of head.

3. Paint pig pink all over, and let dry. Paint eyes on spool end and two dots for nose on end of cork. Put mouth on cork too. Paint flowers and leaves (or other design) on spool body. Let dry.

4. For tail, wind the piece of pipe cleaner around a pencil. Slip it off the pencil and stretch it slightly. Put glue on one end of the tail and push it into the back spool hole.

Ear

Push-Mobile

You Will Need:

4 short spools, the size used for silk thread

4 pieces of cardboard, 8 x 8 inches

2 pieces of dowel stick, each 2 inches long and thin enough to fit loosely in spool holes

4 thumbtacks

tack hammer

fine sandpaper

tracing paper, pencil, scissors, paper punch, glue, paints, brushes

How to Make It:

1. Trace pattern for car (page 62) onto tracing paper and transfer to coardboard. Draw 8 car shapes, then cut them out. Using paper punch, make axle holes where indicated on pattern. Be sure holes are in the same place on every car shape. Spread glue all over one side of a cardboard car and stick it to another car shape. Repeat this until all eight shapes are glued together, one on top of the other. Press car under a stack of books until dry and flat. Now sand all edges smooth and even.

2. Paint car and dowel stick axles a solid color and let dry. Paint spools to look like tires and put windows and door detail on one side of the car. Let paint dry, then turn car over to the other side. Paint on windows and door detail.

3. Now, put car together. Push a dowel stick through one axle hole in car. Slip a spool tire on one end of stick, then hammer a thumbtack into stick end to keep tire on. Put a spool tire on the other end of stick and tack it in place. Push the other axle into other hole; add wheels in the same way. Try designing a car, using your own ideas also.

Spool Top

You Will Need:

2 short spools, the size used for silk thread, or saw a small spool in half crosswise

cardboard

a piece of dowel stick, about 4 inches long and ¼ inch in diameter

small pencil sharpener

compass

pencil, tracing paper, scissors, glue, paints, brushes

How to Make It:

1. Trace pattern No. 1 onto tracing paper and transfer it to cardboard. Do the same thing with pattern No. 2, so you'll have two flower-shaped cardboard pieces. Cut them out with scissors. Then punch a small hole in the center of each shape with a compass point.

2. Sharpen one end of the dowel stick in the pencil sharpener to make a pointed end.

3. Paint one spool, the stick, and flower shape No. 1 a solid color. Paint the other spool and cardboard shape No. 2 another color, and let dry. On one side of each cardboard flower, paint a design using bright colors. Make circles, swirls, dots, or any design you like.

4. Brush glue on one end of a spool and stick it in the middle of flower shape No. 1, matching holes. Put glue on the other spool end and stick flower shape No. 2 on top. Next, paste the other short spool in the center of flower No. 2. Be sure to match all holes. Now, push the dowel stick all the way into the top spool until the pointed end extends 1 inch out of the bottom spool. Make a pencil mark on the stick right below the bottom spool and another mark just above the top spool. Pull the stick out. Spread glue thinly all around the stick between the two pencil marks. Then push the stick back into the spool hole the way you did before. Let dry.

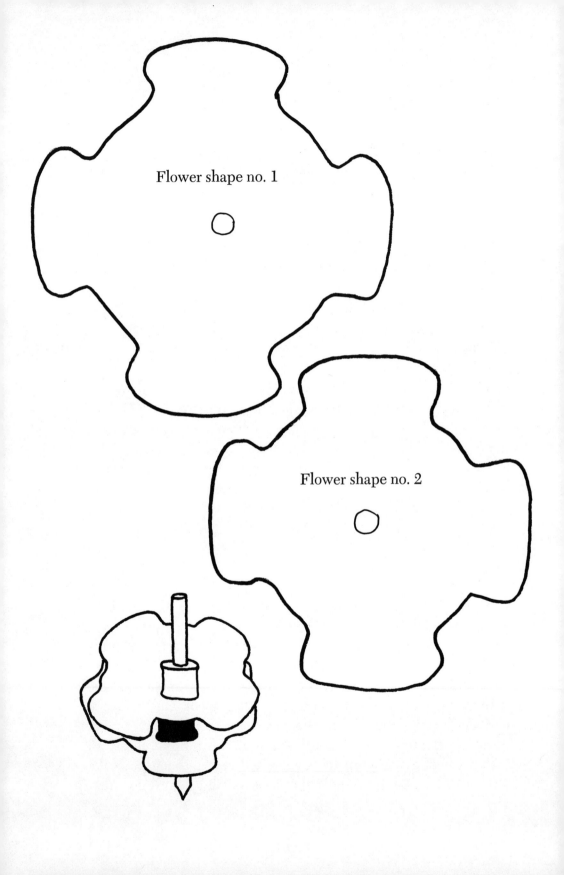

Flower shape no. 1

Flower shape no. 2

Spool Handle Jump Rope

You Will Need:

    4 small spools

    2 large wooden beads from a baby's bead-stringing set

    clothesline, about 2 yards (or as long as you want)

    lollipop or thin dowel stick

    glue, paints, brushes, cellophane tape

How to Make It:

1. Glue two spools one on top of the other. Do the same with the other spools, then glue a bead head on top of each one. Gently push a lollipop stick through both handles to make sure glue has not covered the holes.

2. Paint the spools a solid color and the bead heads a skin color, and let dry. Then paint features on faces and some design on each body. Either copy the clown idea shown or use an idea of your own. Let paint dry.

3. Wrap a piece of cellophane tape around both ends of the rope to give the rope finished ends almost like a shoelace. Push one end of the rope through the bottom of one spool handle until it extends out the top about 3 inches. Tie a knot a few inches from the end, then tie another knot in the rope right under the spool body. Put the other handle on in the same way. Remove the cellophane tape from both ends and unravel the rope by pulling the strands apart. Now your handle figures have hair.

Wrap the rope ends.

Tape

Clown Stick Puppet

You Will Need:

1 large spool (Step 1, Working Techniques)

dowel stick, 8 inches long and ¼ inch in diameter

small amount of knitting yarn for hair

circular piece of bright-colored fabric, 16 inches in diameter

small piece of felt, 3½ inches square

compass

paints, brushes, glue, scissors

How to Make It:

1. Put glue around one end of the dowel stick and push it all the way into the spool hole.

2. Paint the spool head and stick white, and let dry. Paint facial features on top of the solid white coat. A clown's nose and mouth are usually big and red.

3. To make a pompon for the hair: First, hold out two fingers of one hand and spread them apart. With your other hand, wrap yarn around the two fingers about 25 times. Now, slip the yarn off your fingers, holding it together in the middle so the loops won't come apart. It will look like a yarn bow. Tie a short piece of yarn around the center of the bow, then cut through all the loops on each side. Spread some glue on top of the clown's head and

stick on the yarn hair. Arrange the strands so they stick out all over.

4. Set the compass at a 1½-inch radius and draw a circle on the felt, then cut it out with scissors. Fold the circle in half, then in half again. Snip off a small part of the center point and cut off a little corner along the curved edge (see illustration). Open up the circle and this will be a scalloped collar with a hole in the center. For the costume use the circle of bright-colored fabric. Find the center of the fabric circle and snip out a little hole. Slip the felt collar on the puppet stick, then push the stick through the hole in the circle costume. Hold the stick with your hand under the costume close to the head. Now you have a clown puppet who will say something funny every time you do.

Cut off point.

Cut off corner.

Spool Plane

You Will Need:

    1 large spool
    2 tiny spools (the size found in mending kits)
    2 pieces of dowel stick, one 2¼ inches long and ¼ inch in diameter, another 2½ inches long and a little thinner than ¼ inch in diameter
    cardboard
    aluminum foil pan (used for frozen foods)
    3 thumbtacks
    tack hammer
    paper punch
    glue, pencil, tracing paper, scissors, paints, brushes

How to Make It:

1. Brush glue around all but the last ½-inch end of the 2¼-inch dowel stick, then push stick all the way into the large spool, letting ½ inch extend from the front end.

2. Trace the pattern for propeller onto tracing paper (Step 10, Working Techniques) and transfer it to the flat bottom of the aluminum foil pan. Cut the propeller out of aluminum foil. Next, bend the two blades slightly so they tilt in opposite directions and push a thumbtack into propeller at the place marked with a dot on the pattern. Hammer tack into the end of the dowel stick that is extending out of the spool. Don't hammer it all the way in or the propeller won't spin freely.

3. Trace patterns for wing and tail and transfer them to cardboard. Draw two wings and two tails, then cut them out. Spread glue on one tail piece up to the dotted line of the tab. Lay the other tail on top. Don't glue the tabs together because they will be used to attach the tail to the spool body. Spread the tabs open, in opposite directions. Put glue on the tabs and stick tail to the back end of the spool. Next bend wing tabs down, brush glue on tabs, and stick a wing to each side of the spool body.

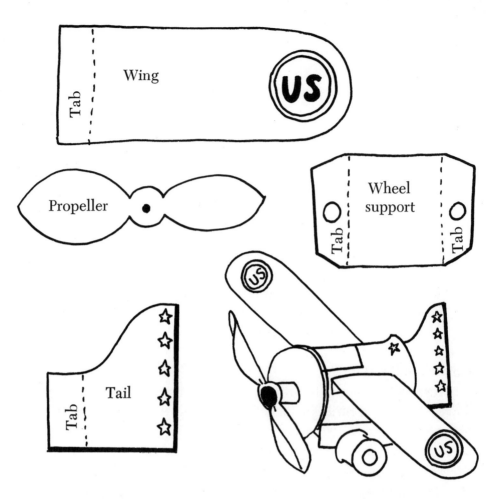

4. Trace pattern for wheel support onto tracing paper and transfer to cardboard. Cut it out, then bend tabs down and punch a hole in each one with a paper punch, where shown on pattern. Brush glue all over the middle section between tabs (but not on tabs) and stick the wheel support to the underside of the spool body.

5. Paint spool plane, the two tiny spools and the other piece of dowel stick. The tiny spools will be the wheels and the stick will be the axle. Paint the plane but not the propeller. Let dry, then paint on an emblem.

6. When paint has dried, push stick axle through holes in wheel support. Slip a spool on one end, then hammer thumbtack into the end of the stick axle. Do the same thing with the other wheel on the other end of the axle.

Flagship

You Will Need:

2 small spools

piece of nicely sanded wood, 6 inches long and 3 inches wide and about ½ inch thick

dowel stick, 5 inches long and ¼ inch in diameter

6 brads (skinny nails), 1 inch long

tack hammer

small saw

strong black carpet thread

scraps of colored construction paper

pencil, ruler, sandpaper, glue, scissors, enamel or acrylic poster paints, brushes, tracing paper

How to Make It:

1. Look at the illustration and follow it as closely as you can. On one 3-inch edge of wood measure and make a pencil dot in the middle of the board, 1½ inches from both side edges. Then make another dot down one long side, 2 inches from the corner. Draw a line from one dot to the other. Do the same thing on the opposite side of board. Using a saw (Step 6, Working Techniques), cut wood on pencil lines to make the pointed bow of the ship. Sand the cut edges smooth.

2. Glue the two spools together, one on top of the other. Then put glue on the bottom of one spool and stick it right in the middle of the boat. Brush glue on one end

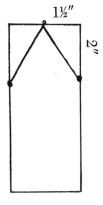

1½″

2″

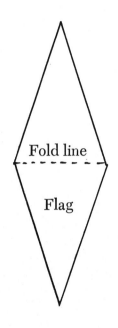

Fold line

Flag

of the dowel stick and push it all the way into the top spool. This will be the mast.

3. To make a railing, hammer brads around the back of the boat. But a brad in each corner and one near the back edge, between the first two nails, 1½ inches from both corners. Then hammer a nail at one side edge 1½ inches from back corner and another in the same place on the opposite side. Finally, put the last nail in the pointed bow.

4. Paint the boat, and let dry.

5. Trace the pattern for flag onto tracing paper and transfer it to colored papers. Draw four flags and cut them out. Fold each flag in half, then glue one around the top of the dowel stick mast. Cut a piece of black thread about 8 inches long. Tie one end to the mast, right under the flag, and the other end to the nail in the bow. Glue three flags, evenly spaced, along the black thread. Cut another piece of thread 10 inches long. Tie one end to the top of a brad at one side of the ship. Pull thread tight and wrap it around the corner nail, then around the next nail and on around the other corner nail. Finally, tie the thread to the last nail, opposite the one you started with. Cut off excess thread and your flagship is ready to sail.

Knitting and Printing
With Spools

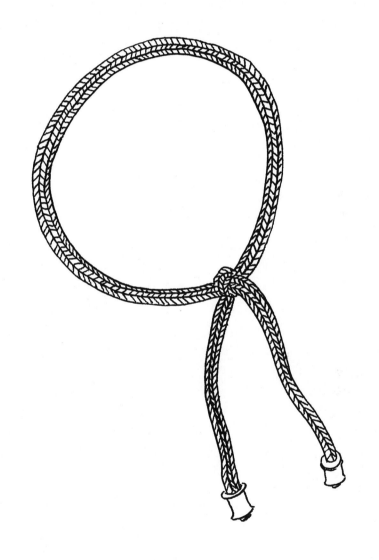

Giraffe Knitting Spool

You Will Need:

    3 small spools
    4 brads, 1 inch long (skinny nails)
    tack hammer
    round file
    4½-inch piece of thin dowel stick
    small pencil sharpener
    glue, paints, brushes

How to Make It:

1. Glue the three spools together, one on top of the other. Gently push the dowel stick through the spools to be sure the glue has not covered the holes. When glue has dried, use the round file to smooth the inside of the spool hole so that when you knit, the yarn horserein will slide through hole more easily.

2. Paint the spools a solid yellow color and let dry. Then paint facial features on one top spool and brown giraffe spots on the other two spools. You could also put on a collar and tie. Let paint dry.

3. Around the hole in the top spool, hammer the four brads until they extend ½ inch above the spool. Place the brads the same distance apart to form a square near the edge of the spool hole.

4. Sharpen one end of the thin dowel stick in the pencil sharpener until it is nicely pointed. This stick will be the knitting needle. Paint the pointed stick a solid yellow color to match the giraffe and let dry. Now you are ready to knit a rope which is called horsereins. With this rope you can make many things, such as a hot mat for your mother. A hot mat is made by coiling and sewing the rope into a flat circle (see page 79). (A dollhouse rug can be made the same way. A rug can be made in an oval or a flat circle shape.)

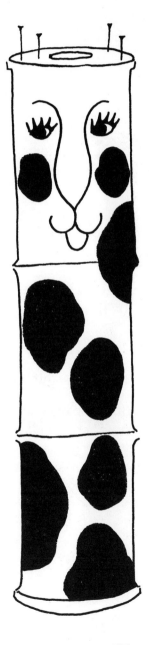

How to Knit with a Spool

You Will Need:
> Giraffe knitting spool and stick needle
> a ball of knitting yarn

Slip knot

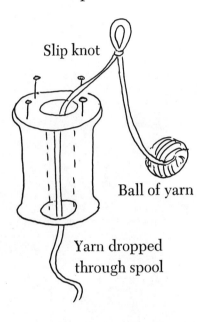

Ball of yarn

Yarn dropped
through spool

Step 2

Wind loop once around
each nail.

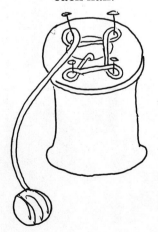

How to Make It:

When you do spool knitting, you work around the top of the knitting spool, making stitches on the four nails. These stitches form a rope which is called horse-reins. As you knit, the horserein forms and goes down through the hole in the spool knitter and comes out the bottom.

1. To knit with your giraffe knitting spool, first drop the loose end of the ball of yarn down through the hole in the spool until it extends out the bottom about 2 inches.

2. Now make a slip knot in the yarn at the *top* of the spool and slip it over one of the nails. Working from *right to left*, take the strand of yarn to the *next* nail and wind yarn *once* around the nail. Do the same thing with the next two nails. This will put a loop on each nail. *Don't pull yarn too tight* or you won't be able to get the loops off the nails. When you are back to the nail with the slip knot, you are ready to knit.

3. Hold the strand of yarn on the *outside* of the nail just above the slip knot. Put the pointed end of your stick needle in the slip knot and lift the slip knot up and over the yarn and off the nail. The stitch you

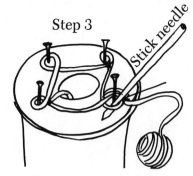

just made will fall behind the nail and slide to the edge of the spool hole. Give the yarn end extending out the bottom of the spool a little tug.

Lift loop up and over yarn, taking it over the nail.

4. Now take yarn strand to the next nail and hold it on the outside of the nail just above the loop that is on the nail. Put the stick needle in the loop and lift loop up and over yarn and off the nail. Tug the yarn at the bottom of the spool again. Do not split the yarn as you work and, above all, keep your work fairly *loose* so that loops lift off easily.

5. Go to the next nail and do the same thing. Continue going around and around the spool, always in the same direction, knitting a stitch over each nail. Keep knitting until the rope is as long as you want it. When you measure the horserein remember also to measure the part that is inside the spool. If you run out of yarn, just tie on another ball of yarn in the same or another color. You can use any odds and ends of yarn and any lengths (if tied together), but always use the same weight of yarn throughout the horserein. For instance, if you start with 4-ply knitting worsted, use only that weight to complete the horserein.

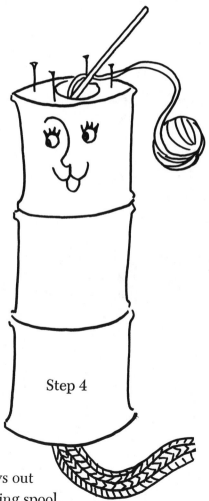

Step 4

Horserein grows out bottom of knitting spool.

How to Bind Off Spool Knitting

1. Cut yarn with scissors leaving a 4-inch end. Thread end into a large-eyed needle. Working from right to left, push needle and yarn through loop on the next nail. Do the same thing with the next three loops.

2. Using your stick needle, lift all four stitches off the nails. Pull yarn (in needle) tight, pulling stitches together. Fasten securely and cut off excess thread. Pull horserein out of spool from the bottom.

3. Now thread the 2-inch end of yard (the piece you dropped down through spool when you first began to knit) into the needle. Push needle into end of horserein and pull it out about 1 inch from end (see illustration). Cut off excess yarn with scissors.

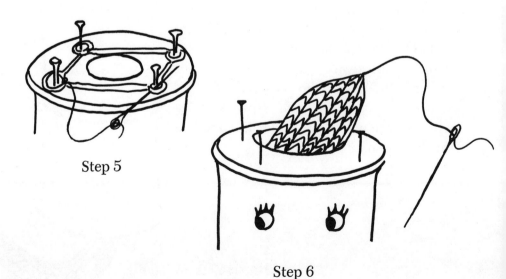

Step 5

Step 6

How to Sew Horsereins Together

1. Lay the two ropes side by side. Thread a sewing needle with a double strand of thread that matches color of yarn and knot the ends. Push needle through a stitch in one rope, then through a stitch in the other rope, exactly opposite the first stitch. Pull needle and thread all the way through. Now, push needle through a stitch below and into the opposite stitch in the other horserein. Continue to go back and forth, from one rope to the other, until the two ropes are joined together.

Knit a Belt

You Will Need:
    knitting spool and needle
    knitting yarn (any color)
    2 small spools
    paints, brushes, glue, tape measure

How to Make It:
1. Paint the two small spools, and let dry. Make them a color to match or contrast with your yarn.
2. Knit a horserein with the yarn until it fits around your waist, then knit about 25 more inches. Bind off your knitting (see page 78). Put glue on one end of the horserein and push it into a small spool. Do the same thing with the other end and the other spool. Your belt is ready to wear.

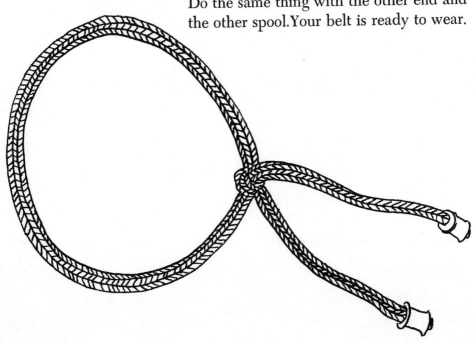

Spool Knitted Santa

You Will Need:

    1 small spool

    2 tiny spools (the size found in mending kits)

    piece of cardboard

    spool knitter and stick needle

    red knitting yarn (worsted)

    red and white sewing thread

    sewing needle

    scraps of red and white felt

    a penny

    tracing paper, pencil, scissors, ruler, straight pins, glue, paints, brushes

How to Make It:

1. Trace pattern for foot onto tracing paper and transfer to cardboard (Step 10, Working Techniques). Draw two feet and cut them out with scissors. Brush glue on one end of a tiny spool and stick it on a cardboard foot near the back edge. Make another boot in the same way.

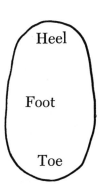

Heel

Foot

Toe

2. Paint boots black and the small spool a skin color, and let dry. Then put facial features on the small spool head.

3. Using spool knitter and red yarn, knit Santa's arms first. Knit a horserein 6 inches long (be sure to include the part inside the spool when you measure the horserein). Put arms aside until body is finished.

4. Now knit a horserein 12 inches long.

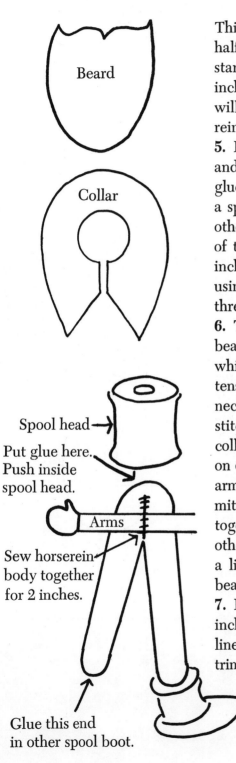

Beard

Collar

Spool head→

Put glue here.
Push inside
spool head.

Arms

Sew horserein
body together
for 2 inches.

Glue this end
in other spool boot.

This will be the body and legs. Fold it in half. Thread needle with red thread and starting at fold, sew rope together for 2½ inches (see page 79). These 2½ inches will be Santa's body; the rest of the horse-reins will be legs.

5. Brush glue on the fold end of the body and push it into bottom of spool head. Put glue on the end of one leg and push it into a spool boot. Do the same thing with the other leg and boot. Now, lay the middle of the arm piece across back of body, ½ inch below head. Sew it securely to body, using running stitches and matching thread.

6. Trace patterns for collar, mitten, and beard onto tracing paper. Pin patterns to white felt and cut out one collar, four mittens, and one beard. Place collar around neck; using white thread, sew three tiny stitches, one on top of the other, across collar front to hold it together. Spread glue on one side of a mitten. Lay the end of an arm on top of wet glue, then place another mitten on top of the arm. Press them all together with your fingers. Attach the other mitten in the same way. Now brush a line of glue along the top edge of the beard and stick it to Santa's face.

7. For suit trim, cut a 2-inch long and ½-inch wide strip from white felt. Brush a line of glue along one long edge and glue trim around body, overlapping the short

Mitten

ends in back of body. Place the trim just above the legs where you finished sewing the body together.

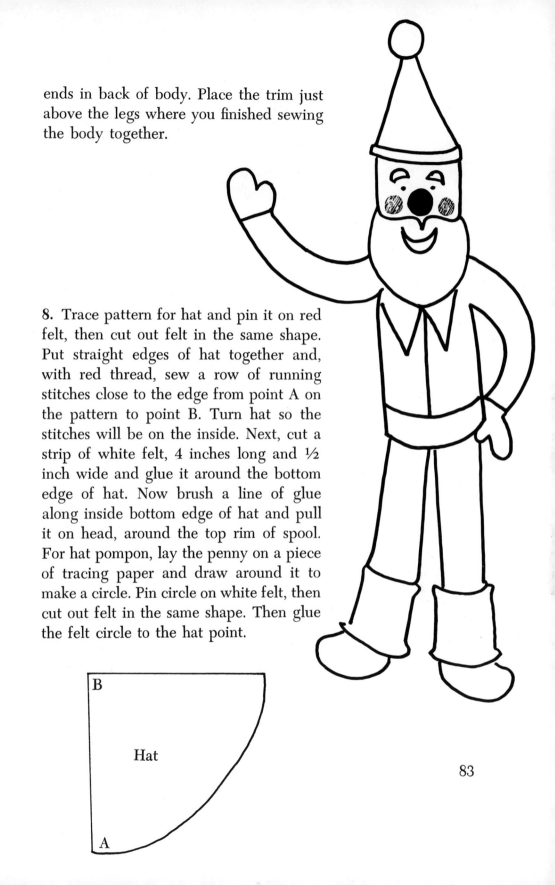

8. Trace pattern for hat and pin it on red felt, then cut out felt in the same shape. Put straight edges of hat together and, with red thread, sew a row of running stitches close to the edge from point A on the pattern to point B. Turn hat so the stitches will be on the inside. Next, cut a strip of white felt, 4 inches long and ½ inch wide and glue it around the bottom edge of hat. Now brush a line of glue along inside bottom edge of hat and pull it on head, around the top rim of spool. For hat pompon, lay the penny on a piece of tracing paper and draw around it to make a circle. Pin circle on white felt, then cut out felt in the same shape. Then glue the felt circle to the hat point.

B

Hat

A

Making Spool Stampers

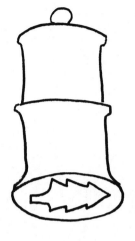

You Will Need:

    small spools

    large spools

    small beads, just a little larger than spool holes

    scraps of felt, thin foam plastic, or ⅛-inch-thick sheet cork

    tracing paper, straight pins, scissors, pencil, glue, paints, brushes

How to Make It:

1. You will need a stamper for each design. Make one, then make others in the same way. Glue a small spool to a large spool, matching holes. Then glue a bead in the small spool hole. These two spools make a stamper.

2. Paint stamper any color you want (Step 3, Working Techniques), but *don't paint the bottom of the large spool.* This is where you will glue the design. Let paint dry and finish with a coat of fixative.

3. Trace one of the designs shown (or one of your own) onto tracing paper. Pin it on felt or foam plastic. Or, if you are using sheet cork, trace and transfer the designs, using carbon paper. Cut out design and glue it to the bottom of the large spool.

4. After glue has dried, paint a black arrow on spool rim just above the *top* of the design. By noting where the arrow is, you avoid printing the design upside down.

Things to Print with Spools

You Will Need:

spool stampers

plain white shelf paper or solid-colored gift wrap, white construction paper and typing paper

pencil with a new eraser

envelopes

narrow ribbon or colored string

scissors, paper punch, regular or acrylic poster paints, brushes, newspaper

How to Make It:

1. *Shelf Paper or Gift Wrapping Paper:* Use plain white shelf paper or solid color gift wrap. You may combine two stampers to make a design like the bell and bow, or use one several times like the holly leaves.

Brush paint on the design shape only.

To stamp on paper, hold stamper straight and press down firmly. Remember the arrow points to top. Practice stamping on newspaper first, and always press stamper on newspaper to remove excess paint from cut-outs before brushing on another color. (The holly berries are made with the pencil eraser.) Always let the first

color dry before adding another color or details. Use a fine paintbrush or pen and ink (black or colored) to add details like sun's face, rays, tree branch.

2. *Gift Tags:* Cut white construction paper into pieces about 4 inches long and 3½ inches wide. Fold pieces in half lengthwise to make a book shape. Punch a hole with paper punch on inside top corner, near the fold. On the cover of tag, print design. Thread a 4-inch piece of narrow ribbon or colored string through hole and tie tag to gift.

3. *Greeting Cards:* Cut card blanks from white construction paper. Make folded, book-shaped cards to fit the envelopes you happen to have. Print design on card front. Print a message with pen and black ink inside after front is dry.

4. *Writing Paper:* Cut white typing paper to fit the envelopes you happen to have. Make single sheets or folded notes which look like small greeting cards. Print design in the top left-hand corner of the paper or print all around the edges for a border design.

5. You can also print tally and place cards, posters, book covers, and unusual storage boxes with your stampers. And, instead of paint, colored ink pads can be used. These can be bought at stationery stores.

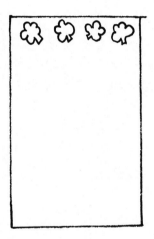

Spool
Games

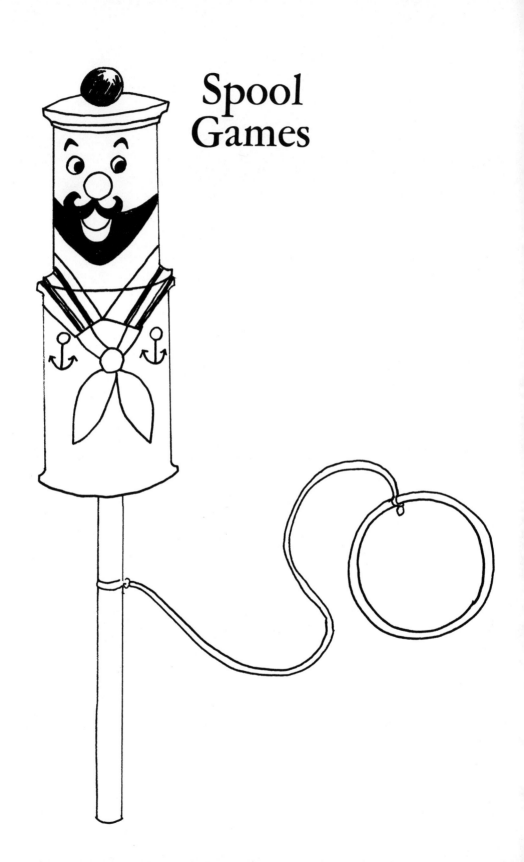

Hot Rod Race

You Will Need:
 2 large spools
 cardboard
 a penny
 8 thumbtacks
 2 large beads
 strong cord or string
 paints, brushes, scissors, pencil, yardstick

How to Make It:
1. Paint the spools a solid color and let dry. Paint a big window on the spools and a number on the front and back of each spool.
2. Put a penny on top of the cardboard and trace around it with a pencil. Do this eight times. These eight circles will be wheels. Cut them out with scissors and paint each one white. Let the paint dry.
3. Push a thumbtack into the center of each circle and stick two wheels to each side of the spool cars.
4. Cut a piece of cord as long as your height. Tie a bead to one end of the cord, then push the other end through one spool car and tie the end to the bottom of a table leg. Cut another piece of cord and do the same thing, but this time tie the cord to another table leg. Now, to have a race with a friend, hold on to the bead end of the cord and pull cord tight. Holding it

waist high, start the cars at the bead end
and gently wiggle the slanted cord to
move them. First one to reach the table leg
is the winner.

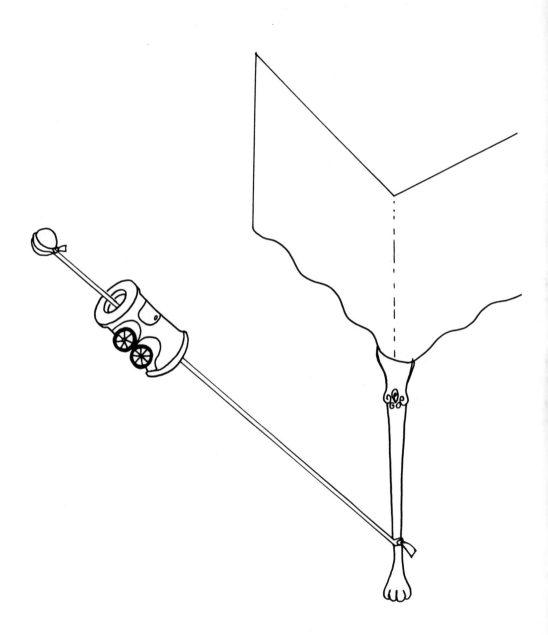

Ring-O-Ling

You Will Need:

    1 small fat spool

    1 medium spool

    piece of dowel stick, 12 inches long and ¼ inch in diameter

    large circular wooden button, about 1½ inches in diameter

    1 medium-sized bead

    a large wooden café curtain ring

    20-inch piece of strong string or cord

    sandpaper, glue, scissors, paints, brushes

How to Make It:

1. Glue small and medium spools together, one on top of the other. The small spool will be the head and the medium spool will be the body. Glue button on top of the small spool for hat. Sand an area on the bead until it is smooth and flat (Step 7, Working Techniques). Then glue the flat side on top of the button. Put glue on one end of dowel stick and push stick all the way into medium spool.

2. Paint spool man, stick, and curtain ring (Step 3, Working Techniques). Make stick a solid color and head spool skin color. Paint button and bead hat a color to match body. Let dry, then paint hair, facial features, and a mustache on face and a design on the body spool (see illustration).

3. Tie one end of the strong string tightly

around the stick about ½ inch below spool body. Put glue around string to keep it from sliding on the stick. Let glue dry. Tie the other end of string to the screw eye in the curtain ring. Tie a knot to make sure the string won't come untied. Hold the stick in your hand, then swing stick, making the ring swing. Flip ring up and over doll's head. This toy is a favorite with children of many lands.

Bowling Set

You Will Need:
    30 small spools
    10 small beads (larger than spool hole)
    small rubber ball about 2 inches in diameter
    glue, paints, brushes

How to Make It:
1. Glue three spools together, one on top of the other. Glue a bead in the top spool hole. You have just made one clown tenpin. Now make nine more.
2. Paint one sailor the way you want him to look. The bead and top rim of the head spool is painted a solid color to look like a hat. The rim of the bottom spool is painted black to give the sailor shoes. Now paint the other nine sailors as you did the first one. When you are finished and the tenpins are dry, set them up and bowl them down.

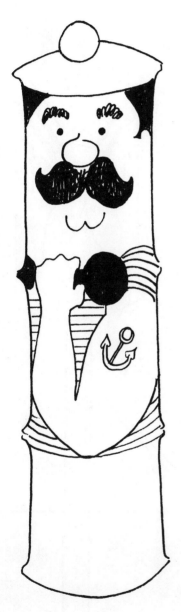

Ring Toss

You Will Need:
    2 medium spools
    4 small spools
    2 extra-large oval or round beads (from a baby's bead-stringing set)
    2 pieces of wood, 2½ inches square and 1 inch thick
    2 circular wooden buttons, about 1 inch in diameter
    2 bottle corks, 1 inch high
    6 plastic bracelets or rubber canning-jar rings
    glue, paints, brushes, sandpaper

How to Make It:
1. Sand pieces of wood (Step 7, Working Techniques). These will be the bases for the ring toss figures. Glue medium spools on center top of bases. Glue two small spools together, then glue the other two together. Glue these on top of each medium spool. The medium spools will be the legs and the small spools will be the bodies of the figures. Now glue an oval bead on each body. Put some glue on the wide end of a bottle cork and stick it right in the middle of a button. Then make another. Glue a button and cork hat on each bead head.
2. Paint figures (Step 3, Working Techniques). Paint the base one solid color, the body and leg spools another color, and the

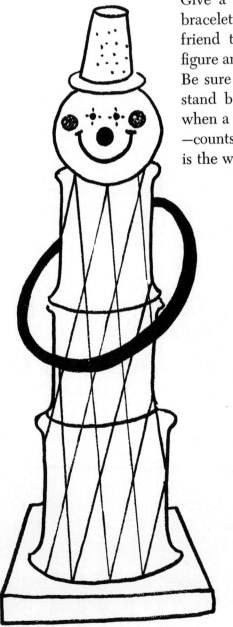

head bead a skin color. Finally, paint the hat, and let dry. Now paint features on the face and make a design all over body and legs.

3. Place the ring toss figures on the floor, facing each other, at least ten feet apart. Give a friend three canning-jar rings or bracelets and keep three for yourself. Your friend tosses his rings over your clown figure and you toss your rings at his clown. Be sure that when you toss the rings you stand behind your own man. A ringer—when a ring falls completely over a clown—counts 5 points. First one to get 25 points is the winner.

Feed the Monkey Game

You Will Need:
>1 medium spool
>a Popsicle stick
>plastic bottle cap (the kind on plastic aspirin bottles)
>a thumbtack
>tack hammer
>a cardboard box with lid, about 14 inches long, 10 inches wide, and 3 inches deep
>piece of brown construction paper
>piece of string, 10 inches long
>cellophane tape, scissors, glue, pencil, paint, brushes
>a bag of peanuts

How to Make It:

1. Lay the middle of the Popsicle stick on the side of the medium spool. Put the thumbtack on top and hammer it all the way through the stick and into the spool, then glue the plastic bottle cap on one end of the stick. This will be the catapult to feed peanuts to the monkey. Paint it (Step 3, Working Techniques), and let dry.

2. Draw a monkey face on the box lid. Make a big round mouth and cut it out with scissors. With the point of your scissors make two holes in the side of the box lid, at the top of the monkey's head. Push ends of the string through holes and tie ends together in a knot to make a hanging loop. Now put glue all over the inside edges of the lid and put lid back on the box. Secure the lid to the box with cellophane tape. Paint the monkey's face, and let dry.

3. Fold the piece of brown construction paper in half and draw a monkey ear on one half of the paper. Make it big (see illustration). Cut out the ear, cutting through both thicknesses of paper to make two ears the same size and shape. Fold back ½ inch

along the straight edge of each ear to make a tab. Put glue on tabs and stick an ear to each side of the box head.

4. Hang the monkey up on the wall. Put the catapult on a table in front of the monkey and place a peanut in the bottle cap, then hit the other end of the Popsicle stick with your fist. Each time a peanut goes into the monkey's mouth, you score 10 points. The first person to score 100 is the winner and gets to keep all the peanuts.

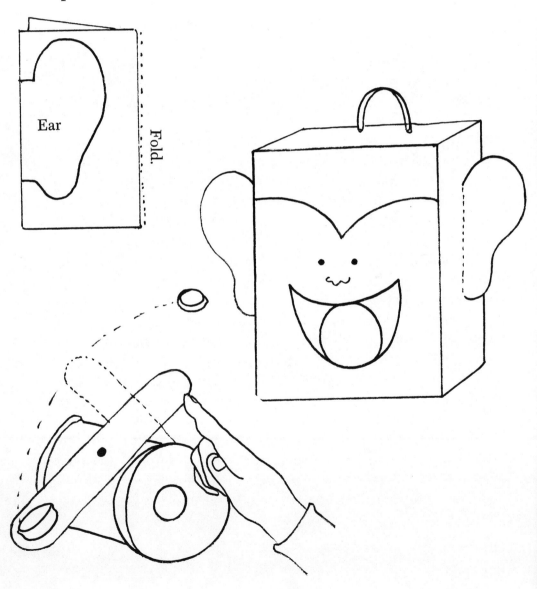

Ear

Fold.

Little People Travel Game

You Will Need:

Road maps, one of your state and two or three of surrounding states (available free from a local gas station)

little people, one for each player (see page 20)

cellophane tape

construction paper

fine-point black felt-tipped marking pen

a very small white tablet

glue, scissors, pencil

How to Make It:

1. Open the state maps and lay them flat on a table. Tape them all together, side by side, to make one large playing board. Plan a travel route across the maps, following highways and roads you find already marked there. Start your route wherever you wish— perhaps in your state at your home town—and end it in another state at a special place of interest or at any town you wish. Use a pencil to trace the route, making it curve, turn, and twist across the playing board. Don't draw the route straight across the maps or the game will end too quickly.

2. Stand a little person on construction paper and trace around it with pencil. You are going to make lots of circles. Cut out circles with scissors. Glue them on the maps over your pencil-traced route. Put circles close together, but not touching, to make a road for the little people to travel on as you play the game. Using the felt-tipped pen, neatly print *Start Here* next to the first circle in your route. Then print *Destination* next to the final circle at the end of the route.

3. You will need 50 playing cards, so tear 50 sheets of paper from the small tablet. Using the felt marker, print *Move 1 Space* on ten sheets of paper, and *Move 2 Spaces* on another ten sheets. Then print *Move 3 Spaces* on five sheets of paper, and *Move 4 Spaces*

99

on another five sheets. Now print *Lose 1 Turn, Stop for Lunch,* on five papers; *Lose 2 Turns, Visit Zoo,* on another five papers; *Go Back 10 Spaces, Took Wrong Road* on five more; and *Move Ahead 10 Spaces, Short Cut,* on the last five.

4. Now you are ready to play the game with your brother or sister or friend (but limit the game to 4 players). Mix up the playing cards and place them face down in a pile. Place the little people at *Start Here*. The first player picks a card and does exactly what it says, moving his little figure along the route on the map. Then he puts his card back at the bottom of the pile. Now the next player takes a card off the top of the pile and moves his little figure along the highway. Continue to play the game by picking cards and moving the little people across the maps. The first person to reach the destination is the winner, but he must pick a card with the correct number of moves to take his figure into the destination circle.

destination

start here ➡ OOOO

Playing cards

Indian Novelties

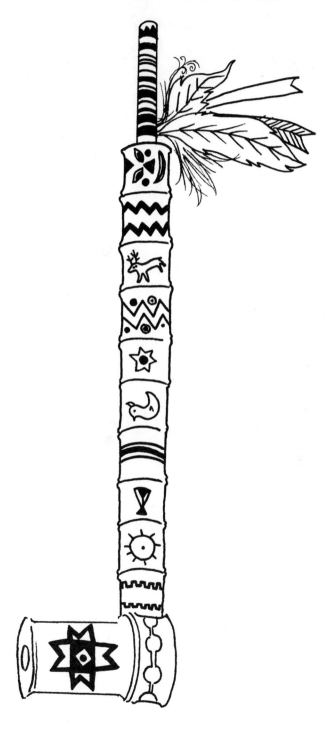

Indian Friendship Stick

You Will Need:
    2 large spools
    dowel stick, 25 inches long and ¼
inch in diameter
    pencil sharpener
    lightweight cardboard
    feathers
    narrow ribbon in bright colors
    3 yellow thumbtacks
    tracing paper
    paints, brushes, glue, scissors, pencil

How to Make It:
1. Glue the two spools together, one on top of the other (Step 2, Working Techniques). Using pencil sharpener, sharpen one end of the dowel stick until it is pointed. This will make the stick easier to push into the ground. Spread glue around the flat end of the stick and push it all the way into the spools. The top spool will be the owl's head and the bottom spool his body.
2. Trace patterns for headpiece and wing onto tracing paper and transfer to cardboard (Step 10, Working Techniques). Make one headpiece and two wings, then cut them out with scissors.
3. Glue the round part of the headpiece on top of the head spool (the dash lines on the pattern show you where to place the spool), then bend point down and glue

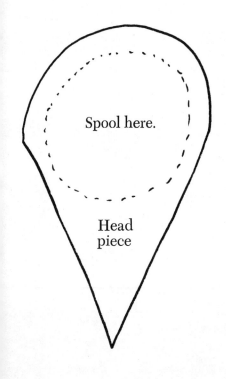

Spool here.

Head
piece

it to the front of the spool. Hold the point in place until glue dries. The headpiece will give the owl his beak and hornlike points on the top sides of the head. Bend the wing tabs back on the dash line, put glue on the tabs and stick them to the sides of the body spool.

4. Paint the stick, spool body, and wings a light brown, the headpiece orange. When paint has dried, make feather design with black paint, over the solid color, using a fine brush.

5. Push the two thumbtacks into the head spool for eyes. Use the other thumbtack to attach feathers and various lengths of ribbon to top of head. Hold some feathers to the stick under the spool body (a little glue will hold them securely to the stick). Wrap and tie ribbon around the feathers. Tie on several lengths of ribbon right under the body.

Friendship sticks were used around Hopi Indian campfires. The stick was presented to a particular person, such as a guest of honor. The person presenting the stick stood before the honored guest and made a little speech voicing good wishes and years of good luck, then pushed the

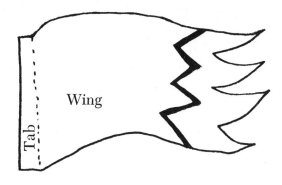

Tab

Wing

pointed end of the stick into the ground near the campfire. Several sticks, some representing wolves, bears, or eagles, were often presented and several speeches given. When the festivities were over, the sticks were gathered together and given to the honored guest as a remembrance of the special campfire ceremonies.

Peace Pipe

You Will Need:
> 10 small spools
> 1 large spool
> 1 round tinker toy piece, the one shaped like a tire with
holes around the sides and one in the middle
> a 14-inch piece of dowel stick, ¼ inch in diameter
> a few feathers
> short pieces of narrow ribbon or colored cord
> glue, paints, brushes

How to Make It:
1. Put glue around one end of the dowel stick and push it all the way into one of the holes in the side of the tinker toy. The dowel stick will be the pipe stem. Brush glue on one end of the large spool and stick it on top of the tinker toy, matching holes. Now glue all the small spools together, one on top of the other (Step 2, Working Techniques). Then, starting at the tinker toy, put glue all around the dowel stick, except for the last two inches, and push it into the stack of spools until the first spool is tight against the tinker toy and large spool. Let glue dry.
2. Paint peace pipe (Step 3, Working Techniques). Let dry. Using black paint and a fine pointed brush, put Indian designs (see illustration) on some of the spools.
3. When paint has dried, glue some feathers to pipe stem just above the last spool. Tie ribbon or cord to stem around top of feathers. Tie on two or three more pieces of ribbon in the same place.

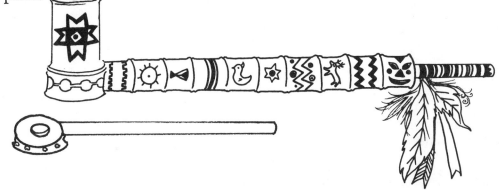

Totem Pole

You Will Need:
    2 large spools
    2 medium spools
    1 small spool
    piece of wood, about 3 x 3 inches and ½ inch thick
    2 wooden picnic forks
    1 Popsicle stick or wooden coffee stirrer
    small saw
    sandpaper, glue, paints, brushes

How to Make It:
1. Glue the two large spools together, one on top of the other (Step 2, Working Techniques). Then glue the two medium spools on top of them, and finally, glue the small spool on the very top. This is the pole.
2. Sand the piece of wood until smooth (Step 7, Working Techniques). This will be the base of the totem pole. Put glue all over the bottom of the large bottom spool and stick the pole right in the middle of the wood base.
3. Using the saw, cut ½ inch off both ends of the Popsicle stick. You will have two small pieces which are ears. Sand the cut edges flat and glue the ears on top of the highest spool on the totem pole. Hold the ears in place until glue is dry. Next saw the handle off each fork. Save one of

the handles for use later. Glue the forks to the back of the top medium spool. This spool will be an owl with wings. Saw a small piece, about 1 inch long, off the remaining piece of Popsicle stick. Sand one edge flat, then sand the other end, rounding off the corners. Glue the flat edge to the front of the next medium spool for a nose. Hold it in place until the glue dries. Give the next spool a beak because it will be a bird. Saw a piece about 1½ inches long off the fork handle, using the rounded end as the bottom of the beak. Hold the beak in position, flat against the next large spool, and put glue on the places where it touches the spool, then hold the beak against the spool until it stays there by itself.

4. Paint the totem pole, making each spool and the base a different color. Let dry. Now paint on facial features, details, and feather markings on the owl's wings. Let paint dry.

Totem poles were carved from very tall trees by the Indians of the northwestern United States. Animal totems were favored by the Indian wood carver.

Kachina Doll

You Will Need:

    2 large spools

    1 medium spool

    a wooden clip clothespin

    2 thin nails, about ¾ inch long

    tack hammer

    Popsicle stick

    1-inch piece of dowel stick, ¼ inch in diameter

    2 small beads

    2 pieces of thin dowel stick, each about 2 inches long and thin enough to fit into the small bead hole

    small fluffy feathers

    small saw, sandpaper, glue, pencil, paints, brushes

How to Make It:

1. Saw the rim off one large spool (Step 6, Working Techniques) and discard rim. Sand the cut edge of spool until smooth and flat (Step 7, Working Techniques). This spool will be the doll's legs. Put glue all over the cut edge and stick the other large spool body on top (Step 2, Working Techniques). Glue the medium spool on top of the body spool. This will be the head.

2. Take the clip clothespin apart by sliding the wood pieces out of the spring grip. Put a pencil mark in the grooves where the spring was. Now, saw each wood piece apart, sawing in the pencil-marked grooves. Discard narrow part of the wood pieces and keep the other two pieces with all the grooves. These will be arms, and the large grooves near the end of each piece will be hands. Sand the cut edges smooth. Place doll on its side. Lay an arm on the side of the body spool. Hammer a nail through top of arm and into spool. *Don't hammer nail all the way in* or arms will not move. Turn doll over and attach an arm to other side of body.

3. Put some glue on one flat end of the 1-inch dowel piece and stick it to the head spool for a nose. Hold it until glue dries. To give the doll ears, saw a ½-inch piece off each rounded end of the Popsicle stick. Glue an ear to each side of the spool head. Brush glue on one end of a 2-inch dowel piece and push it all the way into one of the small beads. Do the same thing with the other 2-inch dowel and small bead. These sticks and beads will be Indian rattles.

4. Paint the doll, using bright colors (Step 3, Working Techniques), following the illustration for costume details and designs. Paint the rattles a solid color and the sticks another color. When paint has dried, glue a rattle in each groove hand before you paint on the clear finishing coat. Let dry. Finally, brush glue on the ends of three or four fluffy feathers and push them into the top of the head spool.

Kachina dolls were made by the Hopi

Indians to represent supernatural spirits. Since the Hopi believed in hundreds of good spirits they made hundreds of dolls, each one just a little different from the other. And each one was named for the spirit it represented. The Kachina dolls were not created as toys but as a way of remembering the names and descriptions of each of the good spirits. They were given to the Hopi children as part of their religious training.

Gifts, Gadgets and Decorations

Jingle Bell Pin

You Will Need:
> 2 small spools
> 2 small jingle bells
> narrow red ribbon
> small sequins
> glue, paints, brushes, scissors, small safety pin

How to Make It:
1. Paint spools green, and let dry. These spools will be bells.
2. Glue a row of small sequins around both spools just above the bottom rim.
3. With scissors, cut a 6-inch piece of ribbon and push one end through the metal loop on one of the jingle bells, then knot the ribbon ends together to make a loop. Next push loop all the way through one of the spools and pull it out of the top of the spool. Pull it again until the knot moves into the spool hole and is hidden. Cut another piece of ribbon and do the same thing with the other spool and jingle bell. Now cut a piece of ribbon 10 inches long. Thread this piece through both ribbon loops extending out of the spools. Tie ribbon into a pretty bow and pin the bells to your coat with the small safety pin.

Pincushion Lady

You Will Need:
1 large spool
1 large wooden drawer pull, about 3 inches in diameter (sold at lumber yards)
jar lid about 2 inches in diameter
circular piece of cotton fabric, in a solid color, about 6 inches in diameter
cotton batting
thread to match the fabric
narrow velvet ribbon
small bunch of tiny artificial flowers
sewing needle, scissors, paints, brushes, glue

How to Make It:
1. Turn the drawer pull upside down and glue the spool on top. The spool will be the head and the drawer pull will be the shoulders of the pincushion. Remove the waxed circle from inside the jar lid, if it has one, then turn it upside down with the inside of the lid facing up. Spread glue on top of the spool head and center the lid on top. The lid will hold the pincushion and be the hat brim.
2. Paint the head, shoulders, and the outside of the jar lid (Step 3, Working Techniques). Do not paint the inside of the jar lid. Let dry, then put facial features and hair on the head and any design you want on the dress.

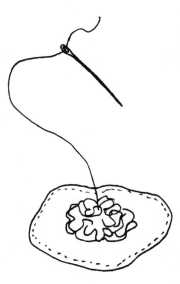

3. Gather the fabric circle at the outer edge with a running stitch (Step 11, Working Techniques). Lay the circle on the table with the wrong side up and place a big ball of cotton batting in the center. Pull up the gathering stitches so that the circle is closed. Pull and shape the circle into a nice round ball.

4. Spread glue all over the inside of the jar lid, then press in the pincushion with the gathering stitches inside the jar lid. You may have to hold the pincushion in place until the glue dries. Tie a piece of velvet ribbon around the edge of the lid in a bow (a few dabs of glue will hold it in place). Take a few flowers out of the bunch and slip the stems behind the bow, then cut off the excess stems. Tie another ribbon bow around the shoulders.

Desk Caddy

You Will Need:

2 small spools

2 small fat spools

4 round, medium-sized beads

a piece of wood, 6 inches long, 3 inches wide, and about ½ inch thick (Step 6, Working Techniques)

small plastic box, about 2 x 2 inches square or any size which will fit easily between the two spools

sandpaper, round file, pencil, glue, paints, brushes

small piece of construction paper, scissors

How to Make It:

1. With the round file, enlarge the holes in all spools (Step 7, Working Techniques) until a pencil will drop through them easily.

2. Lay the board flat on your working surface and glue a bead in each corner for feet (Step 2, Working Techniques). Let glue dry, then turn the board over. Brush glue on one end of a small fat spool and stick it near one back corner of the board. Next glue a small spool head on top, matching the holes. Do the same thing with the other two spools near the other

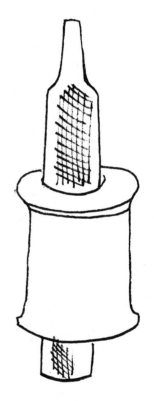

back corner. Lightly sand the outside bottom of the plastic box (sanding will scratch up the smooth surface and help box stick to the wood). Now spread glue all over the bottom of the box and paste it on the board between the spools. Let glue dry.

3. Paint the board and bead feet (Step 3, Working Techniques) a solid color, the fat body spools another color, and the head spools a skin color. Let paint dry, then put on facial features, hair and hat on head spools, arms and clothing detail on body.

4. With scissors, cut a piece of construction paper to fit inside bottom of the plastic box. Spread a thin layer of glue on the inside box bottom and stick on the paper to hide the unpainted wood under the box. Stand a pencil in each of the people spool holders and put some paper clips or rubber bands in the plastic box, and you will have a useful desk caddy.

Spool Sculpture

You Will Need:

1 large spool

1 circular wooden drawer pull, 1½ inches in diameter and about 1 inch thick

tube of plastic wood

molding sticks—toothpicks or thin pointed dowel

pencil, glue, fine sandpaper, paints, brushes

How to Make It:

1. First, turn the drawer pull upside down, then glue the spool on top. The drawer pull will be the shoulders and the spool the head. Think about the character or person you would like to duplicate. You can make him look comical or serious. Now lightly draw a hairline on the spool with a pencil, then fill in the hairline with plastic wood. Apply wood a little at a time (Step 5, Working Techniques), squeezing it from the tube and putting it on the spool with a toothpick. Don't try to cover the head all at one time or the wood will dry before you can mold and shape it. Use a toothpick or pointed stick to push and shape the wood. Cover head with only a thin layer of hair first, then let dry. Apply other layers on top, letting each one dry before putting on the next, until the hair style is built up and finished. Let wood dry.

2. Now put on facial features. Start with the nose. Apply a small lump of plastic wood to face, then shape and mold it into a nose. Let dry. Put on two balls of plastic wood for eyes and shape them; then sketch a mouth on the spool and fill it in with wood. Finally add eyebrows, then ears. Put sculpture aside to dry over night.
3. With fine sandpaper, smooth any rough edges and surfaces. Sand lightly and carefully.
4. Spool sculpture can be painted several ways. Poster paints or enamels can be used if a color effect is desired (Step 3, Working Techniques). An interesting way to finish your sculpture is with bronze or gold enamel spray paints. Or, the wood can be stained with a wood stain, then finished with clear varnish.

Silly Chicken Mobile

You Will Need:

3 small spools (Step 1, Working Techniques)

3 large round beads with big holes (from a baby's bead-stringing set)

piece of dowel stick, 23 inches long and ¼ inch in diameter

small saw

sandpaper

plastic wood

small fluffy feathers

3 small screw eyes

strong black thread, called carpet thread

small brass curtain ring

ruler, pencil, glue, toothpicks, scissors, paints, brushes

How to Make It:

1. All three chickens are made the same way. Make them look different by painting each one a different color. Make one chicken first, then make two more in the same way.

2. Measure and saw a 2¼-inch piece off the dowel stick (Step 6, Working Techniques). Sand one end of the stick until it looks like a newly sharpened pencil. This pointed end will be the chick's beak. Push it into a large bead until the beak extends out about ½ inch. If the stick is too fat to fit the bead hole, sand it until it fits. Make

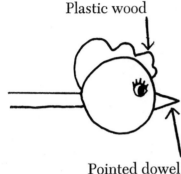

Plastic wood

Pointed dowel

a pencil mark on the stick at each end of the bead, then remove it. Put glue on the stick between the pencil marks (the part that will be inside the bead) and push it back into the bead. Put glue on the other stick end and push it part way into a small spool, letting some of the stick show for the chicken's neck.

3. Squeeze a line of plastic wood from the tube onto the top of the bead head (Step 5, Working Techniques). This will be chick's comb. Let wood set a second, until the surface begins to dry, then using toothpick, shape the plastic wood into a comb. Let wood dry completely. Next insert a small screw eye in top of spool body, up front near the head.

4. Paint chicken (Step 3, Working Techniques). Make the body, head, and neck a solid color, the comb bright red, and the beak orange or yellow, let dry, then put eyes on head. Brush some glue on the ends of three or four small feathers and push them into the back spool hole for tail. Now make two more chickens.

5. To make arms for the mobile, measure and saw off two 3-inch pieces from the dowel stick. The remaining piece will be about 10 inches long. Paint each stick a solid color, and let dry.

6. Now lay the wood pieces on a flat surface, as shown in illustration. Cut a piece of black thread 6 inches long. Tie one end to the middle of piece A, then tie the other end to the long stick at point B. Cut an-

B   E   D

A   C

other piece of thread 6 inches long and tie stick C to the opposite end of the long stick at point D. Cut another piece of thread 6 inches long. Tie one end in the screw eye of a silly chicken and the other end in the middle of dowel stick A. Attach another chicken to stick C in exactly the same way. Now attach the last chicken to the middle of the long stick, at point marked E, using a 14-inch piece of thread. Finally, tie one end of an 8-inch length of thread to the middle of the long stick at point E and the other end to the brass curtain ring. Hang the mobile from a ceiling light, a wooden beam, or any place where it will move and sway. Balance is very important when constructing a mobile, so if you find your mobile will not hang straight, change the position of the hanging threads to find the correct balance points.

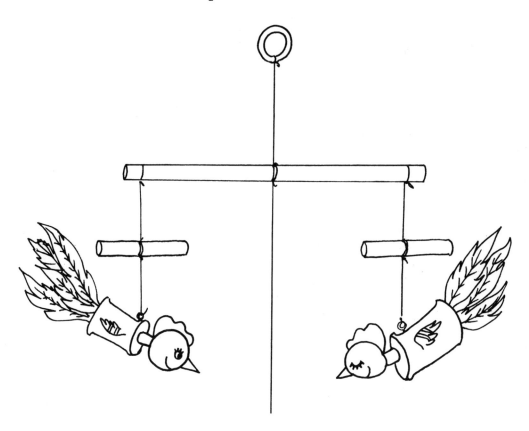

Picture Frame

You Will Need:

    4 small spools, all the same size

    piece of wood, 5¼ inches long, 2 inches wide, and about ½ inch thick (Step 6, Working Techniques)

    small saw

    cardboard, 5 inches long and 3½ inches wide

    piece of clear glass, also 5 inches x 3½ inches (you may have the right size in an old picture frame, or have it cut to size at a hardware store.)

    sandpaper, glue, paints, brushes, ruler

How to Make It:

1. This frame is made for a 3½ x 5 inch photograph. If your picture is smaller, use fewer spools and smaller wood base. If larger, add more spools and make base larger.

2. Saw all spools in half lengthwise and sand all cut edges smooth (Step 7, Working Techniques). About ½ inch from the 3½-inch edge of wood piece, glue one half spool (Step 2, Working Techniques). Glue another half spool ½ inch from the other 3½-inch edge. Put the spools exactly opposite each other with the grooves facing, and put them the same distance from the front and back edges of the board. It will be a good idea, before gluing spools to wood base, to place your photograph in the spool holes, then you will know if you are putting the spools far enough apart or close enough together to hold picture snugly. Now glue all the half spools together, one on top of the other, until your two stacks each contain four half spools.

3. Paint frame and base (Step 3, Working Techniques). Let dry.

4. Place the piece of glass, your photograph, and the cardboard together and slide them into the frame.

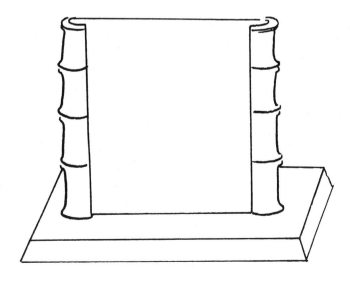

Candy Cart

You Will Need:

   2 short spools (the size used for silk thread) or saw a small spool in half crosswise (Steps 6 and 7, Working Techniques)

   egg carton (cardboard type)

   2 pieces of thick cardboard lollipop stick, each 2½ inches long (or a thin dowel stick)

   a large bead

   3 thumbtacks

   scissors, glue, paints, brushes

How to Make It:

1. Cut one large egg cup out of the egg carton with scissors, then cut the egg cup sides into petals. With the point of the scissors, carefully make a small hole in one side of the cup, near the bottom. Make another hole exactly opposite it in the opposite side of the egg cup.

2. Paint the cup and the two lollipop sticks a solid color (Step 3, Working Techniques), the two small spools and bead another color, and let dry. Then paint a pretty design on the outside of the egg cup.

3. Push a lollipop stick through the holes in the cup. This will be the cart axle. Put a spool on each end of the stick and push a thumbtack into the ends to hold the spool wheels in place.

4. Put glue on one end of the other stick and push it into the bead. This will be the cart handle. From the inside of the egg cup, push the third thumbtack through another side of the cup (which will be the front of the cart) and into the end of the cart handle.

Make other carts in the same way and fill them with candy. Give them to your guests the next time you have a party. Or put a little paper grass in the cart and a decorated egg for an Easter celebration.

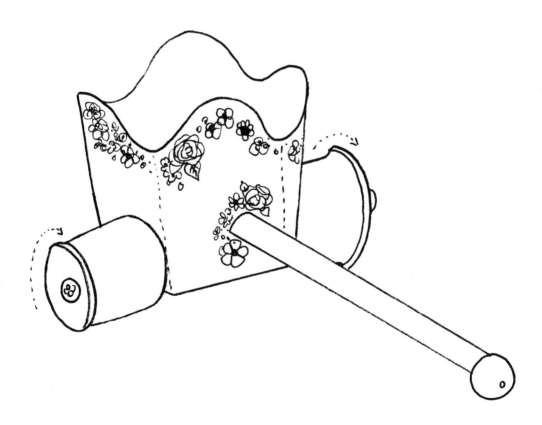

Lollipop Flower Favor

You Will Need:
>1 small spool
>piece of cardboard
>small lollipop
>cellophane tape
>aluminum foil, 4 x 4 inches square
>piece of narrow ribbon, 8 inches long
>tracing paper, pencil, scissors, glue, paints, brushes

How to Make It:
1. Trace patterns for flower and leaf onto tracing paper and transfer them to cardboard (Step 10, Working Techniques). Draw one of each, then cut them out with scissors.
2. Paint spool red (Step 3, Working Techniques) to look like a flowerpot. Make leaf light green and flower shapes any color you wish. Let dry.
3. Put a dot of glue in the center of large flower and stick small flower on top. Then glue flower on front of lollipop (don't take the cellophane wrapping off the lollipop).
4. Wrap the bottom of the lollipop stick with cellophane tape until it fits tightly in the flowerpot spool. Push stick in the hole. Write guest's name on the leaf, then glue it to the stick. Put flowerpot in center of aluminum foil square and bring foil up around pot. Tie a ribbon bow around the foil. Make a lollipop favor for each party guest.

Large flower

Leaf

Small flower

Chris

Uncle Sam Flag Standard

You Will Need:
    2 large spools
    2 circular pieces of cardboard, one 2¼ inches in diameter and the other 3 inches in diameter
        small amount of absorbent cotton
        piece of narrow blue ribbon
        small American flag
        glue, paints, brushes

How to Make It:
1. Put glue on one end of a spool and stick it in the middle of the 3-inch cardboard circle (Step 2, Working Techniques). This spool will be the head. Spread glue on top of head and put the 2¼-inch cardboard circle on top. Be sure to place the circle so that the spool is glued right in the middle. This spool and the small cardboard circle will be the hat and hat brim.
2. Paint the head spool a skin color, but don't paint the bottom rim (Step 3, Working Techniques). Make the hat and hat brim red. The bottom cardboard circle and the bottom rim of the head spool are Uncle Sam's shoulders. Paint them blue. Let dry, then put facial features, white hair, and eyebrows on the head spool, and white vertical stripes on the hat spool.
3. When paint has dried, glue a small piece of absorbent cotton on face for Uncle

Sam's chin beard, and paste the narrow blue ribbon around the hat for a hat band. Insert a small flag in the hat spool. Uncle Sam will be a nice decoration for any patriotic holiday.

Jingle Jester Party Noisemaker

You Will Need:

   1 small spool (Step 1, Working Techniques)
   1 small fat spool
   1 bottle cork, 1 inch tall
   6-inch piece of dowel stick, ¼ inch in diameter
   scrap of cardboard
   5 small jingle bells
   1 glass-head straight pin
   small amount of knitting yarn
   tracing paper, pencil, scissors, paper punch, glue, paints, brushes

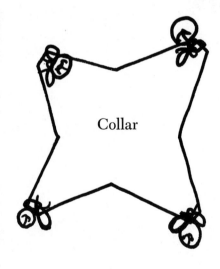

Collar

How to Make It:

1. Glue large end of bottle cork and small spool together (Step 2, Working Techniques). Spool will be the head and the cork will be a hat. Put glue on one end of the dowel stick and push it into the small fat spool. This will be the jester's body.

2. Trace pattern for collar onto tracing paper and transfer it to cardboard (Step 10, Working Techniques), then cut it out. Make holes in each point, where shown on pattern, using paper punch. Glue collar on top of spool body, then paste head on top of collar.

3. Before painting, look at the illustration. You will see that the bottom rim of head spool is part of the collar and painted the same color and the top rim is the hat brim

and will be the same color as the hat. Just the middle of the spool is the head. Paint jester (Step 3, Working Techniques). Use one color for stick and body spool, another for collar, and another for hat. Make head spool a skin color. When paint has dried, put on facial features and hair.

4. Push the pin with the glass head through loop of one jingle bell. Then push it all the way into top of hat. To attach bells to collar, cut knitting yarn into four 4½-inch pieces. Thread yarn through loop of another jingle bell. Push one end of yarn through one of the collar holes and tie yarn into a tiny bow. Attach a bell to each of the other collar holes in the same way.

Candy Cane Elf

You Will Need:
> 1 small spool
> 1 medium spool
> small amount of absorbent cotton
> a tiny candy cane, about 2½ inches
high and ¼ inch in diameter
> piece of thin dowel stick
> glue, paints, brushes

How to Make It:
1. Glue the two spools together, one on top of the other (Step 2, Working Techniques). The small spool will be the head and the medium spool the body. Gently push dowel stick through spool to make sure glue has not covered the hole.
2. Paint the top half of the head spool red (Step 3, Working Techniques) and the bottom half a skin color. Paint the body spool red too, but make the bottom rim black, to give the elf shoes. Let dry, then paint on facial features and white stripes around the top half of the body spool so the elf will wear a red and white striped shirt.
3. When paint has dried, brush a line of glue around the head spool right where the skin color and red hat meet and stick on tiny pieces of absorbent cotton. Do the same thing around the top rim of the body

spool, then the elf will wear a furry collar and a fur-trimmed hat. Push the tiny candy cane into the head spool to complete the hat. (The curved end of the candy cane will be the point of your little elf's hat.)

Golden Ornament

You Will Need:

1 medium spool

a piece of extra heavy aluminum foil (from flat bottom frozen food pan)

4 beads—2 large, 1 medium, and 1 small

sequins (sold at dime stores)

gold metallic cord, about 15 inches long (the kind used for gift wrapping)

gold spray paint, glue, scissors, compass

How to Make It:

1. Set compass at a 1¼-inch radius and draw two circles on the aluminum foil. Cut them out with scissors. Then cut rim of both circles into eight equal sections, like a flower with eight petals (see illustration). Spread glue on each end of the spool and stick a foil circle onto each end (Step 2, Working Techniques). When glue is dry, shape and mold petals slightly around spool, then with a compass point make a hole in the center of each foil circle, matching the hole in the spool.

2. Spray spool and beads gold, let dry, and spray again. When paint has dried, put dots of glue here and there on the spool and press sequins in the glue.

3. Put the two ends of the 15-inch piece of gold cord together and tie a big knot. Push the looped end through the small bead,

Aluminum circle

134

then through the medium bead and one large bead. Next, push the looped end through the spool and on through the other large bead. Now, tie a knot in the cord right at the top of the last bead and you have finished a Christmas tree ornament.

Three Kings Tree Ornaments

You Will Need:

    3 large spools

    construction paper

    small pieces of metallic gift wrapping paper (3 colors)

    assorted small sequins

    3 large beads, larger than spool hole

    silver or gold metallic gift wrapping cord

    small amount of absorbent cotton

    tracing paper

    glue, paints, brushes, scissors, pencil

How to Make It:

All three kings are made alike. You can make them look different by using different colored foil paper for each one and painting each spool head a different skin color. To make the first king:

1. Paint the spool head a skin color (Step 3, Working Techniques), let dry, then put on the facial features.

2. Trace the pattern for the four-sided star onto tracing paper (Step 10, Working Techniques). Put the tracing paper on the other pieces of paper and cut out two foil stars and two construction paper stars. Glue each foil star to a paper star. With the tip of your scissors, make a small hole in the center of each star. Bend the points of each star up, with the foil paper on the outside. Glue sequins on each point.

136

3. Glue one star, with the points facing down, to the bottom of the head spool and the second star, points upward, on top. Match the holes in the stars with the spool holes. Put some glue on the face and stick a small piece of absorbent cotton on for a beard.

4. Cut a 14-inch piece of cord, put the two ends together and tie a big knot. Push the looped end through the spool head from the bottom, slip on a bead, and tie a knot in the cord right at the top of the bead. Now make the other two kings and hang them on the Christmas tree.

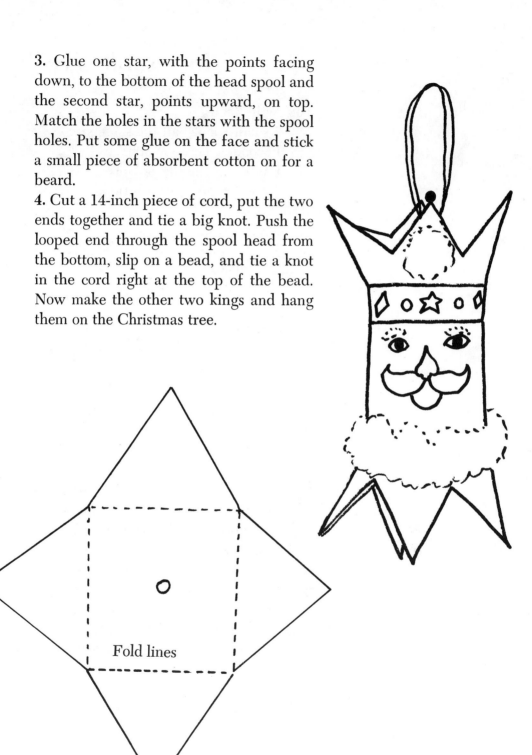

Fold lines

Tiny Table Tree

You Will Need:
7 small spools, all the same size
1 wooden Popsicle stick
1 birthday candle holder
5 small beads, just a little larger than spool holes
1 red birthday candle
circular piece of cardboard, about 3 inches in diameter
glue, paints, brushes

How to Make It:
1. Glue one spool in the center of the cardboard circle, then glue the center of the Popsicle stick flat on top of the spool (Step 2, Working Techniques). This will be the base of the tree. The rest of the tree is a built-up pyramid consisting of three rows of spools.
2. For the first row, glue three spools to the Popsicle stick. The center spool will be right on top of the base spool and there will be about ¾ inch between the center spool and the end spools. Glue two spools for the second row and one spool for the last row as shown in the illustration, putting glue only on edges of the spools where they touch each other. Brush some glue around the bottom of the candle holder and insert it in the top spool, then paste a bead in each of the remaining spool holes.

3. Paint tree green, and paint beads, candle holder, and base red (Step 3, Working Techniques). Let dry. Put the candle in the holder.

Base

Santa Candy Jar

You Will Need:

2 large spools

1 short spool (the size used for silk thread), or saw a small spool in half crosswise. (Steps 6 and 7, Working Techniques)

a small plastic tube with screw-on lid (the same diameter as large spool)

scrap of red construction paper

small amount of absorbent cotton

pencil, scissors, glue, enamel paints, brushes

red hard candies

How to Make It:

1. Put a large spool on red construction paper and trace around with pencil to make a circle. Cut it out, then glue circle to one end of a large spool. Brush glue on the bottom of the plastic tube and stick tube on top of the red paper circle. Brush glue on one end of the other large spool and paste it on top of the lid. The first spool will be Santa's legs, the tube his body, and the spool on top of the lid will be his head. The short spool is Santa's hat; glue it to top of head.

2. Using enamel paints (Step 3, Working Techniques), paint the leg spool black, the head a skin color, and the hat spool and top of the head spool red. Let dry, then paint a black belt with yellow buckle

around the middle of tube, paint on arms and hands, and paint eyes and nose on head.

3. Put some glue on the face and stick on absorbent cotton for a beard. Brush a line of glue around the top rim of head spool and stick on cotton for fur hat trim. Take a small piece of cotton, mold it into a ball and glue it to the top of the hat. Now, fill Santa's body with red hard candies.

Miniature Castle Scene

You Will Need:

1 small spool

1 medium spool

circular cardboard, about 2¼ inches in diameter

egg box, one which has high peaks between the egg cups inside the box

4 round beads—1 small, 1 medium, and 2 big ones

2-inch piece of thin dowel stick, thin enough to fit into a large bead

silver glitter

toothpicks

10-inch piece of silver gift wrapping cord

compass, glue, paints, brushes

How to Make It:

1. With the compass point, make a small hole in the cardboard circle near the edge (Step 9, Working Techniques). You will use this hole to plant a tree.

2. Glue the small spool and medium spool together, one on top of the other (Step 2, Working Techniques). Brush glue on the bottom of medium spool and stick it right in the middle of the cardboard circle. These two spools will be a castle. Put glue around one end of the thin dowel and push it all the way into a large bead. Now brush glue on the other end of the stick and plant tree in the hole you made in the

cardboard circle. Next glue the small bead on the medium bead. If you have trouble making these two beads stick together, get a round toothpick and break off a short piece, then brush glue all over it and push it into the two beads. This will hold them together. Now glue the tiny bead figure on the cardboard circle next to the spool castle.

3. With scissors, cut a tall peaked section out of the egg box. These peaks have four sides. Cut the bottom edge of each side into scallops, giving each one a shape like petals of a flower (see illustration). Make a small hole with compass point in the top of the peak. This peak will be the castle roof.

Cut a tall peak for tower.

EGGS

GRADE A

4. Paint everything with two coats of gesso. When this has dried, paint the spool castle, the cardboard circle, the roof and the tree various colors (Step 3, Working Techniques). Then paint body of the little figure a solid color, the head bead a skin color, and the remaining large bead a solid color. Let dry. Use a small brush for the details of the scene. Make hair and

tiny dot eyes and mouth on the figure, a door on the front of the medium spool, and a window on the small spool. Let dry.

5. Brush dots and dashes of glue here and there on the roof and large bead, then sprinkle silver glitter on the wet glue. Do the same thing with the tree and cardboard circle. Let dry.

6. Put the two ends of the cord together and tie a big knot. Push the looped end through hole in roof from the inside and through the large bead. Tie another knot right above the bead. Now brush glue around the top rim of the small spool and push roof down gently over spool until the inside roof and the spool rim touch. This miniature scene can be hung on the Christmas tree.

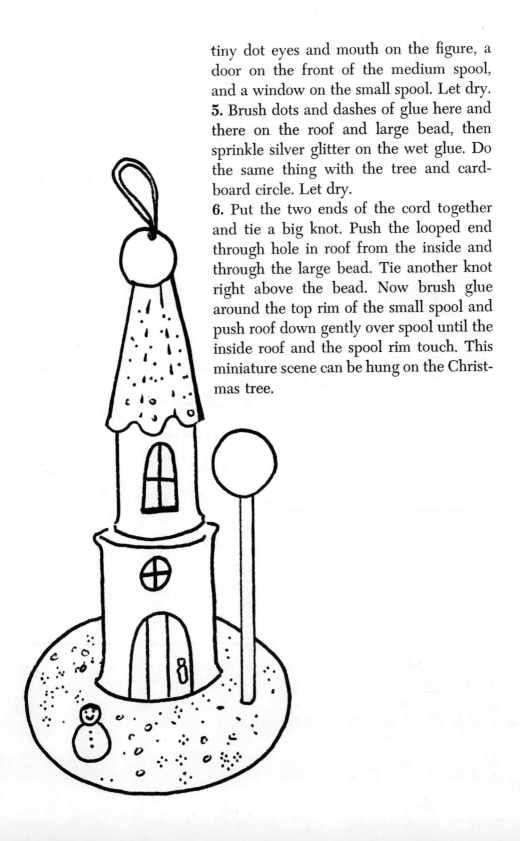

Hanging Christmas Tree

You Will Need:

    a small spool

    2 round beads just a bit larger than spool hole

    green plastic drinking straws

    7 small gold beads

    1 fancy gold bead, a little larger than other gold beads

    metallic gold or heavy-duty green sewing thread

    scissors, sewing needle, ruler, red paint, brush

How to Make It:

1. Paint spool and two round beads red (Step 3, Working Techniques), and let dry.

2. To make tree branches, cut straws into graduated lengths as follows (two straws for each size):

4 inches	2 inches
3½ inches	1½ inches
3 inches	1 inch
2½ inches	½ inch

Lay branches on a flat surface to form a tree shape, starting with the longest straws and ending with the shortest. Thread needle with a 22-inch length of gold or green thread, put ends together and tie a knot. Push needle through one red bead

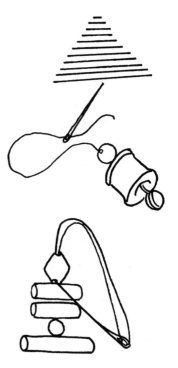

Push needle back through fancy bead.

145

and tie thread around bead. Then push needle through spool and other red bead. Now string on branches, pushing needle through centers of both 4-inch straw pieces and into a gold bead. Next take needle through center of the 3½-inch straws and into another gold bead. Continue threading two branches of the same size, then a bead onto needle, until all straws and small gold beads are used. Finally, push needle through the fancy gold bead, then take needle and thread around bead and push needle through bottom of bead once again. This will tie bead in place. Cut thread right behind needle and knot ends together. Hang tree in a window, from the ceiling, or on the Christmas tree.

Standing Angel

You Will Need:

4 large spools

a circular piece of wood, about 3 inches in diameter and 1 inch high (Step 6, Working Techniques)

cardboard

gold glitter

glue, tracing paper, pencil, scissors, paints, brushes

How to Make It:

1. Glue all the spools together, one on top of the other (Step 2, Working Techniques). Glue the spool stack on top of the circular piece of wood. The top spool will be the head and the other spools and piece of wood will be the body.

2. Trace patterns for sleeve, halo, and wing onto tracing paper and transfer them to cardboard (Step 10, Working Techniques). Make two sleeves, one wing, and one halo, then cut them out with scissors. Bend back the tab of each sleeve, put glue on the tabs and stick a sleeve to each side of top body spool. Fold the cardboard wing in half, brush glue in a straight line on the fold and stick wings to the center back of top body spool. Hold wings in place until the glue dries.

3. Paint angel (Step 3, Working Techniques). Make the head spool and hands a skin color, and the body and sleeves

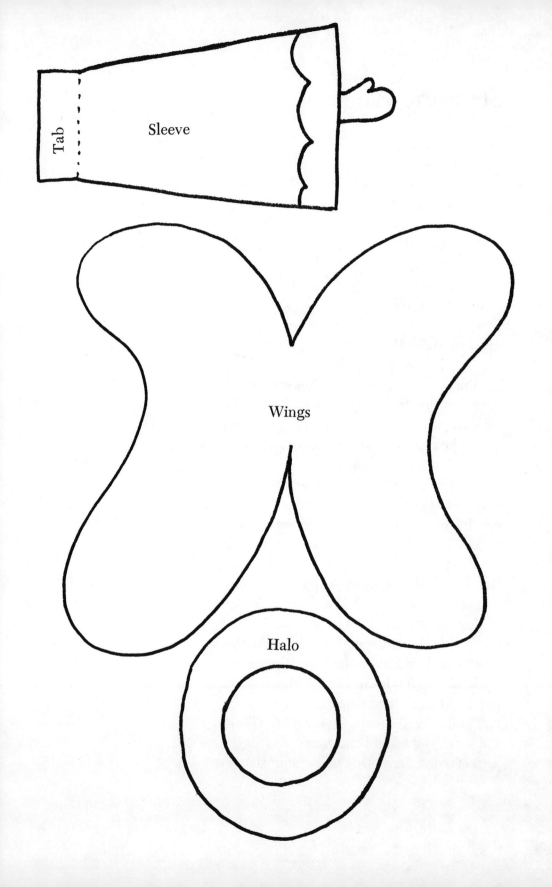

Tab

Sleeve

Wings

Halo

white. Paint wings and halo yellow. When
paint has dried, put a design on the dress
if you wish, and put on hair and facial
features. Before finishing angel with a
clear plastic spray, glue the halo to back
of head, and let dry. Then brush dots of
glue on halo and wings and sprinkle on
gold glitter while glue is still wet. When
angel is dry, spray with clear plastic spray.

The Nativity

You Will Need:

15 small spools (Step 1, Working Techniques)

4 tiny spools (the size found in mending kits)

tube of plastic wood

small plastic tube or bottle caps

circular button

small beads

2 pieces of gold metallic gift wrapping paper, each about 5 inches long and 2 inches wide

small matchbox

yellow tissue paper

toothpicks, glue, paints, brushes, tracing paper, pencil, scissors

How to Make It:

1. All the figures, except the baby Jesus, are made of three small spools glued together, one on top of the other. Top spool will be the head and the other two spools the body. You can start by gluing three spools together to make the figure of Mary (Step 2, Working Techniques). Then do the same thing to make Joseph and the Three Kings. To make the baby Jesus, glue two tiny spools together.

2. Give each figure hair by putting plastic wood on the head spool (Step 5, Working Techniques). Apply small amounts at a time, building up and adding enough

wood to cover the head with a satisfactory hair style. As you finish each King's hair, press plastic bottle cap into the wet wood for a crown, glue beads to top of caps, or paste a cap on the center of a button, then press button into wet plastic wood, or use your own ideas to make crowns. Let plastic wood dry. Next give the Kings and Joseph beards and mustaches. Apply thin lines and tiny amounts of plastic wood to face with a toothpick.

3. Remove drawer from matchbox, discarding the rest. Glue remaining two tiny spools to the bottom of drawer for legs. This will be the crib.

4. Paint figures (Step 3, Working Techniques) the way you think they should look. Paint each King's skin a different color. Paint robes and gowns a solid color. Then, when dry, add details such as sleeve outlines in black and hands the same color as the face. Paint crib brown, and let dry.

5. Glue the two pieces of gold metallic gift wrapping paper together, so you have one piece of paper which is gold on both sides. Trace patterns for halos onto tracing paper, then lay tracing on top of the gold paper and trace over the lines again with pencil. This will transfer patterns by making impressed lines on the foil. Make two large halos and one small halo. Cut them all out with scissors. Now glue a large halo to the back of Mary's head and Joseph's head and the small halo to the back of the baby's head.

6. Finally, fill crib with yellow tissue paper cut into very fine pieces. Place the baby Jesus in the crib and arrange the Nativity scene on a table or mantel.

Sources of Supplies
and Index

Sources of Supplies

Beads:	Kit Kraft 12109 Ventura Place Studio City, California 91604
	Economy Crafts Box 210 Little Neck, New York 11363
	Delco Craft Center, Inc. 30081 Stephenson Highway Madison Heights, Michigan 48071
Cork:	Economy Crafts Address above
	Kit Kraft Address above
Dowel Sticks:	Cardo Sales P.O. Box 1612 Hutchinson, Kansas 67501
	Delco Craft Center, Inc. Address above (Minimum order $5.00)
Feathers:	Kit Kraft Address above
Glitter:	Delco Craft Center, Inc. Address above
	Kit Kraft Address above

The above mail order craft suppliers offer catalogs for a small fee.

Sobo Glue: Slomon's Laboratories, Inc.
                                 43-28 VanDam Street
                                 Long Island City, New York 11101

Sobo may be purchased direct if not available locally.

Acrylic Poster Paints: Rich Art Color Company, Inc.
          and   31 West 21st Street
Gloss Medium: New York, New York 10010

Brochure available. Acrylic poster paints may be purchased direct.

Index

1 2 3 4 5 74 73 72 71 70